THE WALRUS WAS PAUL

*The Great
Beatle Death Clues
of 1969*

ISBN: 0-9646452-1-1

Library of Congress Catalog Card Number: 95-70931

Cover Design: Mary Mazer, Art That Works

Photography by Terry Raby.

Dowling Press wishes to express deep gratitude to Mary Mazer, Janice McCombs, George McCombs, Charline Williams, and Emily Spann.

Dowling Press, Inc.
3200 West End Avenue
Suite 500
Nashville, TN 37203

Additional copies available by calling 1-800-409-7277.
All other inquiries: 615-783-1668

For Shea

CONTENTS

Prologue   vii

Chapter 1   "I Buried Paul": In The Beginning
             The British Invasion And American Mass Media   1

Chapter 2   "I Buried Paul"
             The Search For Conspiracy   11

Chapter 3   "I Buried Paul":
             The Fatal Accident   17

Chapter 4   The Impostor Theory:
             Sgt. Pepper's Lonely Hearts Club Band   33

Chapter 5   *The Magical Mystery Tour*   41

Chapter 6   *The White Album*
             "Here's Another Clue For You All:
             The Walrus Was Paul"   57

Chapter 7   Charles Manson's Helter Skelter, *The White Album*,
             And The Strange Case Of William Campbell   73

Chapter 8   "One And One And One Is Three"
             Come Together   83

Chapter 9   "Number Nine? Number Nine?"
Revolution 9   95

Chapter 10   "Paul Is Dead"
And The Answer Is. . .   113

Chapter 11   The Ultimate Beatle Death Clue Quiz   119

Epilogue   127

Appendix   129

Bibliography   137

PROLOGUE

December 8, 1980, was a typical winter's night in East Tennessee. I had just taken my car to a small mini-mart in Oak Ridge to fill it with gasoline. It was an ordinary Monday. My English Literature classes were struggling with Shakespeare's *Macbeth* and my radio was, as always, blasting out the rock sounds of WIMZ radio. Then, an announcement came over the airway. In a frantic voice, the late night DJ announced that John Lennon had been shot and killed by an assassin. It was approximately 11:45 PM. An old fear that I had felt only once before stirred in my consciousness.

On November 22, 1963, I was in my eighth grade classroom awaiting a scheduled visit to my friendly dentist when the school intercom interrupted my trance-like daydreams of hypodermic needles and novocaine with a stunning announcement: John F. Kennedy had been shot in Dallas and was presumed dead. At the tender age of thirteen, my fears dealt with the uncertainty of the future. Would the cold war become the apocalypse? Why didn't we build that fall-out shelter? Did I have to still go to the dentist?

The networks continually broadcast news about the Kennedy assassination throughout the night. The eerie background of the shroud-like darkness that engulfed the White House stood out in my young mind, and, for a short time, I regressed back into that eighth grade classroom as the same butterflies filled my stomach and silently gave way to the cold nausea that flooded me. President Kennedy's death made me question my future. Where were we going? What would be our fate?

The death of John Lennon was different. There was no all-night vigil. The American people did not hold Kennedy and Lennon in the same high regard. At the time, there was even a movement to have John and Yoko deported. I thought this was ridiculous. What crime had the man committed? This same man sang "Give Peace a Chance" and filled our consciousness with the need for love for all our fellow men. It dawned on me that Lennon's tragic death had a more profound effect upon me than the Kennedy assassination. While Kennedy's death concerned my hope for the future, John Lennon's death signaled the end of my youth.

I will never forget the night of February 9, 1964, as I watched the Beatles perform on *The Ed Sullivan Show*. Like millions of others, I was swept away by the band's overpowering charisma. I immediately rushed out and bought "I Wanna Hold Your Hand" -- an event that would happen each time a new Beatles album was released. I duplicated the Beatle haircut even though my high school adhered to a strict dress code including a rule that boys' hair could not touch their eyebrows, ears, or shirt collars. I began playing the guitar and practiced until my hands were numb. To me, this was the life. All I had to do was grow my hair long, learn the guitar and retire to the screaming sounds of adoring female fans.

I became somewhat successful with the guitar, but found that teaching would become a new passion. As those elusive dreams passed before my eyes once again, I realized that the fleeting idealism of youth was only temporal -- a theme that the death of John Lennon echoed.

That next day at Oliver Springs High School I prepared a memorial for John Lennon. We played Beatle records and interpreted their lyrics. I explained the importance of youth and how each of us should set goals and strive to fulfill those goals. I explained how each of us should charge into life and make our lives count for something. It was difficult listening to Lennon's voice. The emotions were too great and tears filled my eyes. Why this senseless tragedy took place was an answer I was unable to give my students.

I have read that Mark Chapman, Lennon's assassin, was inspired by J.D. Salinger's *The Catcher In The Rye*. Like Holden Caulfield, Chapman presented himself as the savior for the innocence of childhood. Apparently, Chapman had been influenced by Lennon's statement that the Beatles were more popular than Christ. Montesquieu once said that more blood had been shed for Christianity than all the wars in history. It now seemed ironic that the very teachings of Christ became manipulated into a holy quest to rid the world of a man of peace.

I had always hoped the Beatles would get back together for one more concert. Of course, this was only a selfish desire to force the four men who were responsible for so much to give just a little more. But, there was no return to youth; our lives are spent rushing toward the abyss.

A female fan once asked Lennon the question "When are the Beatles getting back together again?" to which Lennon replied, "When are you going back to high school?"

Lennon's Socratic answer was perfect. We can never go home again. The secret of life is to continue and keep growing, to forgive your own mistakes and search for complete happiness.

Thank you John, Paul, George, and Ringo for the pleasure you brought me and countless other fans.

ACKNOWLEDGMENTS

I would like to take this space to acknowledge several works that greatly helped me in my research. First of all, William Dowlding's *Beatle Songs* was a vast resource of material collected from various Beatle interviews and saved me many hours of research. Also, Dowlding listed a series of death clues found in his research.

David Sheff's *Playboy Interviews With John Lennon And Yoko Ono* was fascinating in giving Lennon's remembrances of the development of each Beatle composition. I would also like to mention each of the following highly-recommended works which served as inspiration: Peter Brown and Steven Gaines' *The Love You Make: An Insiders Story of The Beatles;* Nicholas Schaffner's *The Beatles Forever;* Ray Coleman's *Lennon;* Mark Lewisohn's *The Beatles: Recording Sessions;* Hunter Davies' *The Beatles;* Tom Schultheiss' *A Day In The Life: The Beatles Day By Day, 1960-1970;* Chris Salewicz's *McCartney;* Philip Norman's *Shout! The Beatles In Their Own Generation;* Derek Taylor's *It Was Twenty Years Ago Today: The Story of Sgt. Pepper's Lonely Hearts Club Band;* Barbara Suczek's *The Curious Case of The Death of Paul McCartney;* and John Neary's "The Magical McCartney Mystery" for *Life* Magazine.

I would also like to thank these individuals for their help and inspiration: Shea (my beautiful daughter who often complained of being born too late and missing the Beatles, Woodstock, and the excitement of the sixties); Mark Hightower, guardian of the sacred Beatle relics without whose help this effort would not have been possible; Maryglenn McCombs and Dowling Press, Inc.; Mark, Myra, and John of JM Productions; Mark Lapidos and *Beatlefest;* Charles Rosenay and David Schwartz of *Good Day Sunshine* (the World's #1 Beatles fanzine); Ramona Simmons; Kelly and Kevin Hargis; Ben Blanton; David and Varilyn Smith (truly great and supporting friends); Howie and *The Music Machine* in Baltimore; Mark Hughes; Chet Bobin (The #1 Beatles fan from Texas); Jay Nations; Ken Goans; Glenn Neuwirth and "Sea of Timeless Records"; Mike and Maria Armstrong and "Lost and Found Records"; Craig Hampel; Walt Adams of *TNN;* Daisey V. Dunlap; Ted Hall and Kim Stephens of WBIR-TV (Knoxville); Natalie Dick and Russ Murphy of WATE-TV (Knoxville); Wayne Bledsoe of *The Knoxville News Sentinel;* Delores (my muse, wife, and partner without whom this would not have been possible); Denny and my incredible mother, Ruby M. Hunt, (who showed me nothing but unconditional love and unquestioned support); as well as everyone else in my whole family, who was always there for me and gave me much more than I can ever return. This book is written in loving memory of "Two Mamas and Pop" and my father, Rudolph G. Patterson. I would also like to thank the following disc jockeys for their support -- without a doubt the best in the business:

Jim Zippo and J. Fox "The Fox That Rocks" from *The ABC Radio Network;* Cam Gardiner CKLW -- Ontario, Canada; Jeff McKee Richmond's XL-102; Lou and Larry of Des Moines' 95-KGGO; Tim and Mark from Phoenix's 93.3 KDKB (the best Beatle fans anywhere and the best on-air interview. . .hope to see you guys later!); Joe Johnson's *Beatle Brunch,* and *Radio Caroline* in New Zealand.

And finally, to the many fans who are so supportive and continuously suggest more and more clues. Thank you. . .and this book is for you!

DEDICATION

*To my dad, Gentry D. Hunt
Fathers are determined by
much more than chromosomes.
Instead, fathers are determined
by their many unselfish acts
of unconditional love.*

INTRODUCTION

In order to develop a better understanding of the significance of the "Paul Is Dead" rumors, the reader should consider the clues as segments of three major groups:

(1) **The totally ridiculous**: Some of these clues are forced to fit into the mystery as gently as a sledge hammer splintering a round peg into a square hole. A number of these clues are included only through rumor and cannot be confirmed, but many of them are hilarious. I'll leave these for you to decipher. It is, after all, a mystery tour. . .right?

(2) **Guided looking and guided listening**: WARNING: Clues in this category can be the thing nightmares are made of. Once you see the clues or hear the hidden messages in a reversed tape you will never forget it. Pleasant dreams!

(3) **The unexplained**: These clues had to be placed by the Beatles themselves and for what purpose may never be known! Perhaps you can take up the quest and, with this as your guide, solve this incredible puzzle of Beatlemania.

CHAPTER 1

I Buried Paul

The
British
Invasion
and the
American
Mass Media

The Beatles were the musical messiahs of the turbulent sixties. John Lennon, Paul McCartney, George Harrison, and Ringo Starr led the British invasion that finally forced America to surrender. No other British force from Henry Clinton and George Cornwallis to Sir Edward Pakenham accomplished so convincing a victory upon American soil. The method of conquest was not with fire and sword, but with electric guitars, amplifiers and fab songs which brought the Mersey beat into every American household.

American television, that unsuspecting British ally, innocently brought the Beatles into our living rooms February 9, 1964, mainly due to the foresight of Ed Sullivan. But, not even Ed Sullivan, the promoter who brought the American populace Robert Goulet, Elvis, and trained animal acts, could foresee the devastating consequences of such an act. The show had received over 60,000 requests for tickets to the Beatle performance (Schaffner, 14). Though some sources maintain that the television studio's seating capacity was only seven-hundred, eight hundred tickets were given out through an impartial drawing, and those breathless individuals, chosen by fate, would witness the surrender of American youth.

On that peaceful winter night, the home-viewing public was said to have numbered well over seventy-three million Americans and reportedly included none other than the Reverend Billy Graham. Although a veteran of the television wars, Ed Sullivan must have been amazed that this British group had such a high ticket demand. Elvis Presley set the record for the highest number of ticket requested in 1958. Fans of the King requested over 7,000 tickets (Schaffner, 14). This was a foreboding of things to come -- four mop-topped Englishmen had topped the American King of rock and roll!

This new form of rock and roll blazed like wildfire through record stores and television dance shows (e.g. *American Bandstand; Ready, Steady, Go!; Hullabaloo;* and *Shindig*). A new culture and art form was born. The formula was simple; the beat came from the roots of American rhythm and blues. The Beatles -- long-haired Englishmen with London dialects -- modified the musical styles and riffs of famous black artists like Little Richard, Muddy Waters, and Howlin' Wolf -- virtually unknown American music turned into the "new" British sounds the sixties market demanded. This exposure, in essence, helped restore the careers of a number of great black musicians and provided a profitable market for recordings that had been overlooked by previous generations.

The Beatles were the forerunners of this new experiment. Their tight harmonies and melodies helped combat the great loss encountered by a generation fostered on Camelot and the untimely assassination of John Kennedy -- the American President who represented the American dream of endless youth and embedded the growth of hope and opportunity for all. The Beatles influenced the sixties cultural style that brought the American public the Beatle haircut, Nehru jackets, and Cuban heeled boots. New vocabulary terms such as "groovy," "fab," and "gear" helped shape the American vernacular.

Unfortunately, the sixties lost the romantic quest of youthful ideology and turned instead to the certainty of grief and despair. We, as a generation, found that the heroes of our youth were only as mortal as the dreams that transferred them into the quiet sanctity of adulthood. That which seemed timeless ended. The leaders who heard and followed other drummers were cruelly gunned down by assassins' bullets. Men who dreamed great dreams and tried to lead the way to toleration by standing up to the hypocrisy that existed in our society were torn from us as saplings ripped from the Earth by the raging storm.

Rock and roll was not exempt from the tragic fate that laid waste to youthful dreams. Buddy Holly, Ritchie Valens, The Big Bopper, and Eddie Cochran all died tragically at the heights of their fame. On October 12, 1969, it seemed that there was the horrible possibility that Death had stretched out his cold, clammy hand and claimed not just another rock star, but one of the Beatles themselves.

For a number of weeks in 1969, radio call-in lines were backlogged with urgent requests from hysterical fans who demanded an answer to the same question: *Was Paul McCartney dead?*

October 12, 1969, must have started as routinely as any other day. Russ Gibb, disk jockey for Detroit's underground station WKNR-FM, received the phone call that would launch an unprecedented outbreak of hysteria throughout the pop world. The caller, who gave his name only as Tom, suggested that Gibb listen carefully to the fade-outs of certain Beatle songs. As Gibb listened intently, he heard what seemed to be a number of references suggesting that Paul McCartney had met with an untimely end (Schaffner, 129).

Many claim that one of the first written reports of the "Paul Is Dead" hysteria started with an article written by Tim Harper appearing in a college newspaper in Des Moines, Iowa, September 17, 1969. The article, "Is Paul Dead?" also appeared in the *Chicago Sun-Times* on October 21, 1969 (Hockinson, 97).

Not to be outdone, Alex Bennett of radio station WMCA-AM in New York added fuel to this macabre rumor. Bennett followed the alleged clues to London in order to unearth more facts concerning the Beatle tragedy. Bennett was so involved in his pursuit that he stated, "The only way McCartney is going to quell the rumors is by coming up with a set of fingerprints from a 1965 passport which can be compared to his present prints." Bennett presented the so-called evidence to the public through his call-in radio show.

Others became involved in the search for death clues as a wave of hysteria snowballed the American public. Incredibly, there was a television special in which F. Lee Bailey, legendary defense attorney, questioned a number of witnesses including Beatle manager Allen Klein, and Peter Asher, the brother of Jane Asher, Paul McCartney's one time fiancée, and member of the rock group Peter and Gordon. As Klein and Asher denied any and all evidence supporting the conclusion that Paul McCartney had met with a tragic demise, Gibb and fellow investigators presented the grim evidence to the viewing public. The special ended with Bailey's suggestion that the public make up its own mind about the facts. We alone must seek the answer to our own questions based on our own understanding of the purported evidence. Interestingly enough, no video copy of this television special remains. No one seems to remember what happened to the master tapes!

This revelation of evidence revolved around the theory that Paul McCartney was decapitated in an automobile wreck occurring after he left Abbey Road studios angrily, apparently upset over an argument with the other Beatles. McCartney took a ride in his Aston Martin sports car and perished horribly in the ensuing accident. This accident supposedly took place in November, 1966, and most probably on a Tuesday (Schaffner, 127). One version of the tragic accident mentioned a despondent Paul picking up a female hitchhiker who later unknowingly caused the accident by her over-enthusiasm to get closer to the pop icon. The mystery girl's name was supposedly Rita. In "Lovely Rita," McCartney sings, "I took her home. I nearly made it." Many listeners were convinced that this was another reference to the car crash.

According to William J. Dowlding's *Beatle Songs:* "McCartney did have a car crash on a Wednesday at 5 AM. It happened on November 9, 1966, after an all-night recording session, and was coincidentally the morning after John met Yoko" (Dowlding, 158). As his sources, Dowlding cited H.V. Fulpen's *The Beatles: An Illustrated Diary*, and *The Macs: Mike McCartney's Family Album*, written by Michael McCartney, Paul's brother. According to Michael McCartney, Paul had a crash on a motorbike that caused "severe facial injuries to one half of his baby face" (Dowlding, 158).

In *McCartney*, Chris Salewicz gives the following description of the accident: "Late in the year [November, 1966] Paul went up to stay at his father's house for a few days. A friend of both his and John's, Tara Browne, the heir to the Guinness fortune, was already at the house as a guest of Mike McCartney's. One evening, after smoking a joint, Paul and Tara decided to take out a pair of mopeds and ride over to visit a member of the Mac clan, Aunt Bett. Close to his aunt's home, Paul took a corner too fast and soared over the handlebars, landing on his face and badly cutting his upper lip. To minimize publicity, the family doctor was called and the wound was stitched up. The heavy mustache grown for the *Sgt. Pepper's* LP helped hide the scar until it healed properly" (Salewicz, 183).

The biggest problem with the theory that suggested Paul's death resulted from an automobile accident, not the simple motorbike crash, dealt with the police reports that most assuredly had to be filed concerning such a serious charge as an unreported death. Surely there were records -- a death certificate or autopsy report -- that could substantiate this bizarre occurrence.

Another unanswered question dealt with the lack of eyewitnesses. Such an extraordinary occurrence would have proved lucrative for any ghoulish spectator willing to cash in on his or her privileged knowledge of the disastrous event.

On October 14, 1969, two days after the rumor broke on WKNR-FM, the *Michigan Daily* ran a review of the latest Beatle album, *Abbey Road.* The review, written by Fred LaBour took the form of an obituary, illustrated with a gruesome likeness of Paul's severed head (Schaffner, 129).

Fad songs with titles such as "St. Paul" by Terry Knight, later producer of Grand Funk Railroad, the ghoulish "Paulbearer," "So Long Paul," recorded by a young Jose Feliciano under the pseudonym Werbley Finster, and "Brother Paul," by Billy Shears and The All-Americans, were released in timely fashion. "Brother Paul" was released by WTIX, a New Orleans radio station and had an advanced order of 40,000 copies in the New Orleans area alone (Hockinson, 99). It appeared that a dead Paul McCartney made for very good business!

It was unimaginable that the American public easily accepted such an unfounded rumor. However, this same generation had been raised on the questionable authority of the infamous Warren Commission Report concerning the investigation of John F. Kennedy's assassination. We, as a generation, began to dispute what we were told. If a conspiracy hiding the facts of an American President's murder existed, then it would not be out of the realm of possibility to suggest that the death of Paul McCartney could be hidden from the public. In 1968, America lost Bobby Kennedy and Martin Luther King, Jr., to the tragic, untimely deaths that many experts believed were the results of other conspiracies. We questioned everything. We trusted no one -- especially those over thirty.

The Beatles had left the safe road of simple love songs and turned to the quest for social awareness. They strongly opposed the war in Vietnam, admitted their use of marijuana and LSD, and John Lennon had even suggested that the Beatles were more popular than Jesus Christ: "Christianity will go. It will vanish and shrink. I needn't argue about that. I'm right and will be proved right. We're more popular than Jesus Christ now. I don't know which will go first, rock 'n' roll or Christianity. Jesus was all right, but his disciples were thick and ordinary. It's them twisting it that ruins it for me" (Schaffner, 57).

Apparently, John Lennon and the other Beatles were deluged with requests to perform Christ-like healings of their sick fans. In the January 7, 1971, issue of *Rolling Stone,* Lennon stated: "Whenever we were on tour in Britain, everywhere we went, there were always a few seats laid aside for cripples and people in wheelchairs. . . .the mothers would push them at you like you were Christ or something, or as if there were some aura about you which would rub off on them. . . .it seemed like we were surrounded by cripples and blind people all the time, and when we would go through corridors, they would all be touching us and things like that. It was horrifying."

Possibly, the experience of the Beatles being relegated toward sainthood drove John away from the precepts of organized religion and into the cynicism he now embraced. Eventually, under the urging of Brian Epstein, Lennon claimed that he had been misunderstood (about the Beatles being more popular than Christ) and that his words were taken out of context. Epstein claimed that John had only expressed his deep concern for the "decline in interest of religion."

Barbara Suczek makes reference to this interest in the decline of religion in "The Curious Case of The Death of Paul McCartney." The following is from an interview with a fourteen-year-old freshman (male) in November 1969:

"Well, I hate to say it, but Jesus doesn't turn me on like the Beatles do. I feel like a hypocrite, but I think John Lennon was right when he said that [the Beatles were more popular than Christ]. I get turned on by our church group, though. Like when we sit around together and discuss *Galatians* and we're all together and you really turn on. Like you love everybody -- feel close to everybody. . . .the Beatles are good. They tell the truth. They believe in love and people. They're against hypocrisy. They turn you on."

The sixties generation desperately needed something to believe in. *Playboy* created a furor when they released statements by the Beatles detailing other questionable beliefs and made the masses realize for the first time the Beatles weren't the boys next door.

The Fab Four not only attacked religion, but sexual mores, as well. Most of us were also stunned when the Beatles turned to Far Eastern religious practices to further their search for absolute truths and inner peace. They chose their own spiritual guide and guru in the Maharishi, while John stated that he now considered himself a Buddhist. Along with

----

the members of the Beach Boys, Donovan, and Mick Jagger, the Beatles studied under the Maharishi and received their mantras. George Harrison stated, "Each person's life pulsates in a certain rhythm, so they give you a word or sound known as a mantra, which pulsates with that rhythm. By using the mantra. . .to transcend to the subtlest level. . .the mantra becomes more subtle and more subtle, until finally you've lost even the mantra, and then you find yourself at the level of pure consciousness" (Schaffner, 87).

It seemed that the Beatles no longer only wanted to hold our hands; they wanted to turn us on! The Beatles first became spiritually aware at the Maharishi's conference in Bangor, Wales. They also chose to follow him for a more detailed workshop at his retreat in Rishikesh, India. It was here that the Beatles, with the possible exception of George Harrison, became disenchanted with the Maharishi. One by one the Beatles left India. Ringo, the first to leave, claimed that the camp reminded him of Butlin's (the British holiday camp for working class children) and that the food was too spicy. Next, Paul McCartney and his fiancée Jane Asher left the camp and stated that the Maharishi was a "nice fellow" but that they were "just not going out with him anymore." John Lennon, however, was probably the most bitter and even composed a scathing song in the guru's honor. This composition was originally entitled "Maharishi"; however, John changed the title, as well as the character's sex, to "Sexy Sadie." It seemed that the giggling guru had an interest in Mia Farrow that John Lennon could not consider exactly spiritual. John wrote: "Sexy Sadie, what have you done, you made a fool of everyone" (Schaffner, 88).

Far Eastern influences permeated the Beatles recordings from 1965 to 1967 like the pungent aroma of incense. George Harrison introduced the droning sounds of the sitar which embellished Beatle compositions. For the first time, the Beatles experimented with backward recordings and introduced metaphysical themes. However, not everyone was happy with this sudden change in the group.

The American public, it seemed, refused to allow change in its heroes. If there were a change in the Beatles, then there had to be an answer for that ominous break. After the release of the Beatle albums from 1967 to 1969, those adoring fans of the past became the inquisitors of the present. A scape goat was demanded as some sacrificial rite, and when the "Paul Is Dead" rumors surfaced in October, 1969, those fans filled with insecurity were only too eager to search for the clues that provided the answer for this strange change in the Beatles' behavior.

The answer was obvious: Paul McCartney had indeed died and an impostor had taken his place.

CHAPTER 2

I Buried Paul

The
Search
For
Conspiracy

As the public absorbed the many clues to Paul McCartney's supposed death, the first and most obvious task was to examine the mysterious conspiracy. This was not an incredible challenge. Since "the love of money is the root of all evil" (and a man needs roots) the villain had to be either the Beatles themselves or the hated Establishment that was created and ruled by the profiteers.

The Beatles performed their last concert as a group at Candlestick Park in San Francisco on August 29, 1966. The Fab Four became reclusive and seldom appeared in public. They rejected great sums of money to perform live as a group once more. The Beatles had become bored with their own notoriety.

According to Ringo, "It was the worst and best time of my life. The best time because we played a lot of good music and had a lot of good times. The worst time . . . where it was like 24 hours a day, without a break: press, people fighting to get into your hotel room, climbing 25 stories up drainpipes. And it never stopped . . . if it had carried on, I personally would have gone insane" (Schaffner, 59).

Not every one of the Beatles was convinced about the "good music" to which Ringo referred. In a *Music Maker* interview, John Lennon exclaimed: "I can't stand listening to most of our early stuff. . songs like 'Eight Days A Week' and 'She Loves You' sound like big drags to me now. I turn the radio off if they're ever on" (Schaffner, 59).

It seemed that the Beatles had given all they possibly could to rock and roll and now they simply wanted to rest and then change direction. Beatle albums continued to be released, but with no live tours to support them. The Beatles now started to think of the album as a continued art form of many great songs and not just a showcase of a few

---

hit singles surrounded by album filler. This concept influenced Brian Wilson of the Beach Boys to achieve a similar goal with the result being the release of *Pet Sounds*, the album that greatly influenced the Beatles' own *Sgt. Pepper's Lonely Hearts Club Band.*

Now, the making of surrealistic and impressionistic film fascinated the Beatles. There were no live performances, which may have been due in part to the heavily-layered orchestral music in their later compositions. The Beatles tried to compensate for the lack of live performances by releasing film versions of their new hits. These releases included "Hello Goodbye," "Penny Lane," and "Strawberry Fields Forever." The group even financed their own British television film entitled *Magical Mystery Tour.* This, however, proved to be a monetary disappointment to the band.

The public somewhat accepted the Beatles' withdrawal from the limelight. If there were to be no more live Beatle concerts, then at least their fans could still enjoy their music and catch a glimpse of their performances through their avant-garde films. But, this strange disappearance only added fire to the death rumors of Paul McCartney.

The public had grown accustomed to the eccentric behavior of popular artists. We were only too aware of Elvis' nightmare existence in Memphis, Tennessee. Presley's rental of movie theaters and whole amusement parks after closing time were common knowledge to fans of rock and roll. Fame, it seemed, was not without cost and sacrifice. With this in mind, most of us forgave the Beatles for their desertion from our imprisoning ideals.

The stigma of Big Business cast a far more suspicious and ominous reflection upon the death clue hysteria. The business community was concerned only with profit. It cared little about the health and well-being of its victims. History provided many examples of ruthless business practices -- the Muckrakers of the Progressive Era developed the exposés that resulted in governmental overseeing of financial empires. There were the Andrew Carnegies, J.P. Morgans, John D. Rockefeller (whom Andrew Carnegie nicknamed "Wreck a fellow" and stated that the Rockefeller motto was "Let Us Prey") and Cornelius Vanderbilt whose family motto became "The Public Be Damned." Obviously these men, and those like them, were the real ogres behind all our problems.

The 19th Century answer to the "sweat shop" was all-night recording sessions, more frequent due dates for album releases, and the soul-tearing grind of merciless, endless touring, and a complete disregard for privacy. The Beatles had indeed been imprisoned behind the glittering golden dollar signs of excess.

Life magazine proposed an interesting theory in its November 7, 1969, issue entitled "The Magical McCartney Mystery," written by John Neary. If the rumors were true that Paul McCartney had died in a mysterious automobile accident, then perhaps the Beatles' management, record companies, and publishing companies conspired to cover up his untimely death. Paul McCartney, dubbed "the cute Beatle," was extremely popular. The question that faced the Beatle interest would now be the continued sale of record albums. Would the public accept a replacement for one of the English messiahs?

The Beach Boys had replaced Brian Wilson with Glenn Campbell during one of their tours, before settling on Bruce Johnson as a permanent replacement. Wilson had undergone a nervous breakdown and a drug dependency that necessitated such a change. But, the Beach Boys seemed to lose the old magic of "I Get Around" and "Surfer Girl." The Rolling Stones had replaced Brian Jones, following his tragic death, with Mick Taylor. Taylor was an incredible talent, but the music again was just not the same. Though the Stones produced, and continue to produce great music, the fire of "Jumpin' Jack Flash" and "Satisfaction" was not rekindled.

With these examples in mind, the risk may have proved too great. Album sales would continue at all costs. Surely, the remaining Beatles could continue their music behind locked studio doors and contribute to the conspiracy that now hid the death of McCartney. After all, the Beatles stood to gain tremendous sums of money from the royalties of future albums. But, what if the Beatles were not profiteers? What if the Beatles were true to their fans?

The group had unquestionably undergone a metamorphosis; somehow they would spread the word to the true believers and warn an unsuspecting public of the grisly facts. These revelations manifested themselves in a series of cryptic clues. The clues were shrouded in the lyrics of Beatle songs. Other clues were hidden on Beatle album covers. All fans had to do was to look carefully, have a good imagination, a fair knowledge of Far Eastern and mythological symbolism, and most importantly, have the money to purchase the albums in question. The search was on and the answers were forthcoming.

CHAPTER 3

I Buried Paul
The Fatal Accident:

Wednesday Morning
at five o'clock as
the day begins.

"She's Leaving Home"

On June 1, 1967, the Beatles released *Sgt. Pepper's Lonely Hearts Club Band.* Possibly no other album in history brought about as much change in musical direction than this work. It was a new era filled with psychedelic sounds that drenched our imaginations in shades of fluorescent colors and pulsating rhythms. After the first week, the album had sold over 250,000 units. In the United States, advance sales numbered one million units, and after three months, American sales reached an amazing 2.5 million. By mid-1987, the album's 20th anniversary, *Sgt. Pepper's Lonely Hearts Club Band* had sold 15 million copies (Dowlding, 153).

Paul McCartney was convinced that *Sgt. Pepper's* was a great artistic album and insisted that the album's cover should match that greatness. After all, the album took more than seven hundred hours to record and cost about $75,000 (Dowlding, 154). Accordingly, the cover was incredible. Peter Blake, who created the artwork for the album, stated: "Paul explained [that the concept] was like a band you might see in a park. So the cover shot could be a photograph of them as though they were a town band finishing a concert in a park, playing on a bandstand with a municipal flower bed next to it, with a crowd of people around them. I think my main contribution was to decide that if we made the crowd a certain way, the people in it could be anybody."

The Beatles did not want just anyone to be among the crowd. The cast included such famous and infamous characters as Marilyn Monroe, Aleister Crowley (The Beast 666), Mae West, Edgar Allen Poe, Oliver Hardy, Karl Marx, Lewis Carroll, Johnny Weissmuller, and Shirley Temple. When the Beatles' management sought releases from the individuals pictured on the album cover, Mae West responded, "What

---

would I be doing in a lonely heart's club band?" All four Beatles wrote West personal letters detailing how much they wanted her to appear on the album. Mae West then agreed and took her place on the cover with the other notables (Dowlding, 157).

Not all of the Beatles' choices made it to the cover, however. John Lennon had suggested that Ghandi, Jesus Christ, and Hitler be included. Through the intervention of Brian Epstein and EMI records, those suggestions were denied. Possibly the Beatle management remembered the public's reaction to Lennon's remarks that the Beatles were more popular than Christ. Therefore, it was important not to offend the Christians, Indians, and Jews, and those disputed figures were removed from the set. Actor Leo Gorcey, one of the Bowery Boys, was taken out of the scene when he demanded a fee. Originally, Gorcey was positioned between the Vargas girl and fellow Bowery Boy, Huntz Hall.

On the cover, the Beatles stood dressed in band uniforms, all in distinctly different colors, gathering around a bass drum bearing the album title. Each band member held a different instrument. These instruments required a total of four hours of careful polishing (Dowlding, 157). It seemed that such a visual masterpiece required strict detail to even the smallest items. Everything was planned to even the most minuscule of details.

Supposedly, many people thought that the group had planted marijuana plants around the bass drum, which was later denied. Though marijuana may not have been planted on the album cover, the fab foursome freely used the drug within the confines of the Abbey Road Studios. Sir Joseph Lockwood, EMI Records managing director stated: "I knew there was some possible connection with cannabis in the studios -- smells were noted -- but I never pursued it. I had a pretty close relationship with the Beatles, largely because they were so successful" (Dowlding, 154).

George Martin, the Beatles' record producer, noted: "Of course I knew they were smoking [marijuana]. They tried to hide it from me; they'd go out into the canteen one at a time. Neil [Aspinall] and Mal [Evans] would have the joints already rolled out there. They'd come back and it would be obvious, but it seemed to help and they had an enormous enthusiasm for recording in those days" (Dowlding, 155).

Ironically, it was Bob Dylan who introduced the Beatles to the drug culture. Dylan had met the group on their American tour in 1964 and introduced the foursome to the mind-expanding consciousness of the mysterious weed. Lennon stated: "He [Dylan] thought 'I Wanna Hold Your Hand' when it goes, can't hide -- he thought we were singing 'I get high' -- so he turns up -- and turns us on, and we had the biggest laugh" (Schaffner, 45). Reportedly, Dylan had a memorable reaction when he first heard *Sgt. Pepper's Lonely Hearts Club Band.* The singer supposedly stated: "Turn that off!" (Dowlding, 163).

As death clue investigators pored ever-so-cautiously over each minuscule detail of the *Sgt. Pepper's* album cover, a number of surprising and bizarre images appeared. The group stood in the center of the montage. Immediately to the right of the performers stood their wax figures, the same effigies that resided in Madame Tussaud's museum. The Beatle likenesses were dressed in the fab style of the sixties -- ties, collarless jackets, the famous hairstyle, but for some reason the infamous haircut now appeared too conservative. American culture had changed so dramatically that even those individuals over 30 now wore longer hairstyles that made even the Beatle look of 1964 rather conservative.

The wax-figures stood together next to the likeness of Sonny Liston, and gazed downward toward the freshly-dug grave covered in red hyacinths which spelled out "Beatles." Peter Blake offered this description from the liner notes of the *Sgt. Pepper's* CD edition: "I wanted to have the waxworks of the Beatles because I thought that they might be looking at Sgt. Pepper's band too. The boy who delivered the floral display asked if he could contribute by making a guitar out of hyacinths, and the little girl wearing the 'Welcome the Rolling Stones' sweatshirt was a cloth figure of Shirley Temple, the shirt coming from Michael Cooper's young son, Adam. The Beatles arrived during the evening of March 30. We had a drink, they got dressed and we did the session. It took about three hours in all, including the shots for the centre-fold and back cover. I'm not sure how much it all cost. One reads exaggerated figures. I think Robert Fraser [photographer] was paid 1500 pounds by EMI, and I got about 200 pounds. People say to me, 'You must have made a lot of money on it' but I didn't because Robert signed away the copyright. But it has never mattered too much because it was such a wonderful thing to have done."

The cover photograph offered a number of sinister explanations. The spectators, perhaps, represented the mourners at a funeral. It did not take long to ascertain that the beautiful yellow hyacinth flowers were in the shape of a guitar -- a left-handed bass guitar, McCartney's instrument.

The presence of Stu Sutcliffe in the crowd may suggest that the instrument placed on the grave actually belonged to him. Sutcliffe, the first Beatle bassist and Lennon's best friend, died of a brain hemorrhage in Germany. If the viewer looked carefully, and used a little imagination, he may be able to make out the macabre message "Paul?" from the hyacinth plants. Onlookers also noticed that there were only three black strings on the instrument. Was the a reference to the three mourning Beatles? Now it was more than evident that McCartney was entombed in the flower enshrouded grave.

The flower "BEATLES" also represented a clue to the many onlookers. (Some onlookers believed that they could make out the numeral three before "Beatles." Could this suggest the three surviving members?)

Many fans noticed that the phrase "Beatles" spelled out in red hyacinths may have suggested that those figures present were only some of the band members (perhaps along with a very lucky impostor). Also interesting is that on a number of later Beatle albums (*Magical Mystery Tour, Abbey Road,* and *Let It Be)* the band refers to itself as "Beatles," as opposed to "The Beatles." To many investigators, it appeared that by not labeling themselves as *The* Beatles, the group gave one more clue that the band was not in its original formation.

The blood-red hyacinth message read "BE AT LESO." The obscure 'o' helped form the enigmatic name of a certain Greek Island, said to be purchased by the Beatles themselves for the final resting place of Paul McCartney. To make matters even more complicated, this incredible island was said to have been underwater. Perhaps overzealous fans combined the myth of McCartney's death to the ancient wonder of another sunken island -- Atlantis. As mentioned earlier, some clues bordered on the ridiculous and could not possibly hold water. But, then again, maybe the island was converted into a home for legendary performers who many believed faked their own deaths. The inhabitants could have included James Dean, Jim Morrison, and a now-tan Elvis waiting for his comeback tour in 2001!

Strangely, at the 1995 Chicago *Beatlefest,* Alistor Taylor mentioned a bizarre story in which John Lennon had asked him to purchase an island. The next day, he saw an advertisement offering an island for sale. One wonders, perhaps, if Lennon named this island "Leso" or if this were merely another one of Lennon's gags.

Issy Bonn, a British comedian and a member of the crowd who adorned the album jacket had his right hand raised above Paul McCartney's head. Supposedly, in certain Far Eastern societies, an upraised hand held over the head of a subject was a symbol of death, or a symbol of benediction. At the very least, McCartney was singled out from the others in this strange manner.

While McCartney stood under the open hand, three of the performers (John, Ringo, and George) held bright, golden band instruments. McCartney, on the other hand, held a black clarinet. Symbolically, black has always represented mourning or death. Another clue presented on the album cover concerned the doll placed at George Harrison's left which looked down upon the grave. The curly-haired Shirley Temple doll wore a striped "Welcome the Rolling Stones" sweatshirt. This intent to plug the Rolling Stones was rather obvious, and the Stones later returned the favor by placing the Beatles' likenesses among the shrubs on *Her Satanic Majesties Request.*. But, under closer examination, investigators noticed a small model car resting on the doll's right leg. This model car strongly resembled an Aston Martin, the mysterious car McCartney supposedly drove on the ill-fated night of November 9, 1966, the date of his purported accident. The doll sat in the lap of a macabre grandmother figure wearing what appeared to be a blood-stained driving glove on the left hand.

Investigators also took delight in noticing a flower-like arrangement peculiarly resembling a flaming car pushed headfirst into the grave. The Indian goddess Kali was placed directly front center of the album jacket. Kali, an Eastern religious symbol of rebirth and regeneration, was described in G.A. Gaskell's *Dictionary Of All Scriptures And Myths* as "a symbol of the present period and process of evolution in which wisdom and love are gradually developed from ignorance and desire. This period of evolution of spirit from matter commences from the death of the Archetypal man (Krishna)."

In this case, McCartney could have symbolically joined the ranks of literary heroes who died young and were later reborn as Gods. He would become another Achilles or Alexander who raised himself to even greater fame in death. This may have paralleled Lennon's statement that the Beatles were more popular than Christ. Only this time Lennon could have answered his fundamentalist detractors through symbolic images. In this symbolic state McCartney may have represented a Christ-figure born again not for the spiritual redemption of mankind, but raised like the Phoenix from the ashes of ignorance and intolerance to lead the way to wisdom and love. This was 1967, and San Francisco was in the midst of the summer of love celebration and all things were possible.

John Lennon was strongly influenced by Lewis Carroll: "My influences are tremendous, from Lewis Carroll to Oscar Wilde to tough little kids that used to live next to me who ended up in prison and things like that" (Scheff, 140). It seemed that the Beatles shared the same passion for word play that Carroll used as a staple in his works.

With Carroll's *Through The Looking Glass* in mind, I experimented with a small, flat mirror held at an angle to the *Sgt. Pepper's* album cover. I became interested in the bass drum when I read that the designer was a mysterious Joe Ephgrave. The last name surely was a combination of "epitaph" and "grave." With this in mind, the bass drum transformed into an eerie headstone for a fallen Beatle.

The bass drum skin looked, at first, innocent enough with the album title psychedelically etched across its surface. The two phrases "Sgt. Pepper's" and "Club Band" were angled to the top and bottom of the drumhead and in similar design. The phrase "Lonely Hearts" was of a different design and was placed in the center and in psychedelic print. The different pattern appeared awkward. Why wasn't the same lettering used for the complete album title?

By holding the mirror perpendicular to the cover and in the dead center of "Lonely Hearts," a hidden message appeared between the glass and cover. The message read: "I One IX <> He Die." Between the words "he" and "die" was a diamond shaped arrow pointing upward to McCartney!

At first the "nine" was obscure. Initially, I assumed it meant that the Beatle with nine letters in his name had died, which fit nicely since only McCartney's contained the needed nine letters.

Dissatisfied with this explanation, I sought an answer to the first mark, the "I One." I read the phrase over and over as "one one nine he die," which was extremely frustrating until I realized that, unlike in mathematics, one and one must not always equal two. In this case, one and one was eleven!

Now the phrase was "Eleven Nine He <> Die" and the answer was obvious. The bass drum became the true tombstone and revealed the exact date of death: November the ninth -- the eleventh month and ninth day.

As mentioned earlier, there is evidence to support the theory that Paul McCartney had been involved in an accident on November 9, 1966. The incredible revelation, however, was that some wanted us to believe that McCartney had died and the album jacket simply served as an obituary to the unsuspecting world.

But, the mystery did not end there! The hidden message in the bass drum may have been designed only for American audiences. The European method for dates places the day followed by the month and then the year. In this case, the message would appear to an English audience as "NINE ONE ONE" or September the eleventh. Of course, had the emergency 911 network existed at that time it would have supplied yet another incredible clue to Paul's death.

In the open album jacket, the Beatles appeared in close up still dressed in their Sgt. Pepper's uniforms. On his left arm, McCartney's wore an arm patch which read "OPD." While in the United State an individual who has died in an accident and been rushed to the nearest hospital is pronounced "Dead On Arrival" or "DOA," in England, the corresponding term is "OPD" or "Officially Pronounced Dead" -- the exact phrase which adorned McCartney's left arm. Paul McCartney later answered the critics' interpretation of the arm patch with a statement suggesting that the Beatles obtained the insignia in Canada and that it could "possibly" have stood for "Ontario Police Department."

Actually, the patch represented Ontario Provincial Police (OPP), yet is seemed odd that McCartney would forget the exact letting of the infamous badge, especially in trying to discredit any sinister connotation. Also in the center section of the album jacket, McCartney is the only Beatle sitting in what many fans quickly interpreted as the fetal position -- the same manner in which ancient Celts buried their dead.

The pulses of sleuths must have raced feverishly upon looking at the back of the *Sgt. Pepper's Lonely Hearts Club Band* album cover. The most noticeable clue was McCartney posed with his back to the camera while the other Beatles faced the lens with stern expressions. Again, this signified that McCartney was singled out and portrayed differently from the others.

The album jacket's back side was in bright red, which led many to think that this represented the accidental spilling of McCartney's blood.

This was also the first time in history that an album's lyrics were included with the recording and this was unusual. The title that appeared across Paul's back was the song "Within You Without You," a song penned by George Harrison, containing the lyrics: "We were talking -- about the space between us all and the people who hide themselves behind a wall of illusion never glimpse the truth -- then it's far too late -- when they pass away." This lyric appeared to be prophetic. Who were these "people who hid themselves behind a wall of illusion"? What was the mysterious "truth"? Yet again, who had "passed away"? Did this mean that the Beatles would go on with Paul or without him?

Since it was George's song, it was appropriate that he should reveal the hidden meaning. Harrison stood to McCartney's right. As he faced the photographer, George pointed somberly to a superimposed line from "She's Leaving Home." The lyric read: "Wednesday morning at five o'clock as the day begins." To ensure the validity of the accident theory, researchers consulted a calendar from 1966 and found that November 9, 1966, was indeed a Wednesday and that McCartney's accident had occurred at 5:00 AM (Dowlding, 158).

One surprising bit of information concerning Paul's alleged involvement in a tragic automobile accident is reportedly found in the *Beatles Book Monthly,* February, 1967. The article mentions a rumor circulating through London stating that on January 7, 1967, the roads around London became icy and very dangerous. Late that afternoon it was reported that Paul McCartney had been killed in a car crash on the M1 Motorway. As this supposition fueled a hysterical outpouring from Beatle fans, one of the Beatles' press agents placed a call to Paul at his St. John Wood home. The Beatle confirmed that he had been home all day and had not left the house. Since there was no truth to the report, the story died there. What is peculiar to the story, however, is the time frame. Since the *Sgt. Pepper's* album was in the early stages of infancy, could this hysteria have been the catalyst for Paul and the other Beatles to plant the "Paul Is Dead" rumors? Obviously, after the many frantic calls seeking the truth about Paul's accident, the Beatles would have been aware of such an incredible marketing strategy. All they had to do was present the story in detailed, yet cryptic clues, to the unsuspecting world! Remember, *Sgt. Pepper's* was released in Great Britain on June 1, 1967, and in the United States on June 2, 1967, thus leaving plenty of time to create the world's greatest hoax.

Upon closer examination, onlookers noticed that the Beatles had placed their epaulets upon their left shoulders, said to be the proper attire for military honor guards at state funerals. Interestingly, the Beatles had consciously changed the epaulets from their right to left shoulders, which is evident by comparing the front and back LP covers. It is also interesting to note that the term 'epaulet' contains Paul's name (ePAULet). Also, Paul wears three black buttons on his jacket. Could this be symbolic of the three surviving Beatles who mourned their partner's tragic end?

Other clues hinting about tragic deaths through automobile accidents were hidden within Beatle song lyrics, the most prevalent of which was found in *Sgt. Pepper's* haunting "A Day In The Life." According to John Lennon: " I was reading the paper one day and noticed two stories. One was about the Guinness heir who killed himself in a car. That was the main headline story. He died in London in a car crash. On the next page was a story about four thousand pot holes in the streets of Blackburn, Lancashire, that needed to be filled. Paul's contribution was the beautiful little lick, "I'd love to turn you on," that he'd had floating around in his head and couldn't use. I thought it was a damn good piece of work" (Sheff, 163).

The Guinness heir that Lennon referred to was Tara Browne, the same figure who was with Paul at the time of his moped accident, and was a friend of the Beatles and other English groups. On December 18, 1966, Browne sped through red traffic lights at 110 mph in his Lotus Elan and smashed into the back of a van parked in South Kensington. He was dead at the age of twenty-one (Dowlding, 179-80).

As to the line "I'd love to turn you on," McCartney stated: "I remember being very conscious of the words 'I'd love to turn you on' and thinking, 'Well, that's about as risqué as we dare get at this point.' Well, the BBC banned it" (*Playboy*, December, 1984).

In the song lyrics to "A Day In The Life," Lennon sings: "I read the news today, oh boy, about some lucky man who made the grade, and though the news was rather sad, well, I just had to laugh. I saw the photograph. He blew his mind out in a car. He didn't notice that the lights had changed. A crowd of people stood and stared. They'd seen his face before. Nobody was really sure if he was from the House of Lords."

Obviously, the death in question had to concern that of an individual who was extremely well known. In Peter Brown and Stephen Gaines' *The Love You Make: An Insider's Story of the Beatles*, the authors referred to this scene: "It was actually John Lennon who 'blew his mind out in a 'car.' John and Terry Doran were driving into London from Weybridge one night with John at the wheel, so stoned on acid he couldn't figure out if the traffic light had changed" (Brown & Gaines, 373).

The "crowd of people" who "stood and stared" may have represented an older generation who had seen the face of the dead man somewhere -- probably in the newspapers or on television -- but couldn't readily identify the corpse. The ghoulish term "nobody" may have been used to describe the body as a victim of decapitation ("blew his mind out") and, in grim humor, allude to the fact that the head had "no body."

In prehistoric times and in many tribal societies, the head was considered to be the receptacle of the spirit (Cirlot, 78). If the head were removed, the spirit could then be freed and, in this case, perhaps bring about a transition to the idealistic concepts of wisdom and love contained in a higher plane of existence. This grim irony would fit Lennon's statement that he "just had to laugh" at the rather sad news in the newspaper. The meaning behind this phrase suggested Lennon's awareness of the humor hidden behind his carefully chosen words. If "a crowd of people stood and stared" at the body, this line could refer to the *Sgt. Pepper's* art work, containing the crowd of people, and fellow celebrities, who now served as members of a wake.

The crowd gathered around a grave has ghoulishly identified the victim for the viewer. However, the record-buying public knew that being a Beatle was much more prestigious than being a simple member of the House of Lords. Many clue-seekers were convinced that Lennon actually sang: "Nobody was really sure if he was from the House Of Paul." Again, this could be another episode of simple coincidence, but this lyric seemed to fit the phrase more closely than the cover lyric sheet which stated "nobody was really sure if he was from the House of Lords."

After the public was made aware of the car crash clue from "A Day In The Life," fans were prompted to ponder lyrics from past Beatle recordings. The Beatle album *Help!* showed McCartney as the only Beatle without a hat -- yet again Paul portrayed differently than his fellow bandmates.

The album *Rubber Soul* now induced images of screaming tires (rubber) and death (soul). As the images were placed together, many sleuths now thought that McCartney had died during the making of this album. It seemed irrelevant that the album was released in the UK on

December 3, 1965, and in the United States on December 6, 1965, almost a year before the tragic accident was said to have occurred. Now it seemed that these new-found mourners searched for any and all clues that would help shed new light upon the McCartney mystery. By this point, some of us saw only what we wanted to see and heard only what we wanted to hear. Most people completely ignored Lennon's comment that the album title came from a pun on "English soul" (Dowlding, 113). The death clue answer made much more sense.

There could well be another pun interpreted as yet another clue to McCartney's death. The *Sgt. Pepper's* LP flip-side contains the first mention of Apple. The Beatles note that this side of the album cover was designed by M.C. Productions and the Apple. The M.C. productions could well refer to McCartney, while "apple," when divided into two syllables, forms another cryptic clue. The first syllable, the prefix 'a', means "without" (e.g., areligious, apolitical, etc.). When the prefix 'a' is used in front of the second syllable, 'pple' the phrase could be translated as 'a - pple' or "without Paul."

The American release of *The Beatles Yesterday And Today* in June, 1966, supposedly contained other clues to McCartney's tragic death. John Lennon described the controversy behind the jacket: "The original cover was the Beatles in white coats with figs 'n' dead bits of meat and dolls cut up. It was inspired by our boredom and resentment at having to do another photo session and another Beatle thing. We were sick to death of it. Also, the photographer was into Dali and making surreal pictures. That combination produced that cover" (Sheff, 194).

The cover was deemed in poor taste by the Beatle management and a substitute photograph was pasted directly over the offending picture. The new album jacket displayed the group posed by an open trunk. Paul McCartney sat inside the trunk, interpreted by many fans as an open coffin -- especially when the album was turned on its side.

To the most ardent believers of Beatle conspiracy, the album photo represented the ultimate theory of a cover-up since the original art was recalled and a new photo pasted hastily in its place. What was the true purpose of such an act? Did the "Butcher Cover" suggest other clues to Paul's demise?

On the cover, Paul is sitting in the middle of the first row between John and Ringo, and is surrounded on either side by headless dolls. Paul laughingly grips one of the doll's heads in his lap while George tries to place another doll's head upon a headless body. To some onlookers this was another clue to Paul's accident. Also, it is interesting to note a pair of false teeth upon Paul's right forearm. To the more persistent seekers of the truth, this clue reinforced a cryptic passage in "Revolution 9": "So any and all, he went to see the dentist instead, who gave him a pair of teeth, which wasn't any good at all."

The very title *Yesterday and Today* may have suggested that the photo represented the Beatles as we remembered them in the past (yesterday), whereas this photograph portrayed the group as they are today with an impostor taking the place of Paul. A number of song titles themselves suggested an eerie reference to the supposed rumor. The album opened with "Drive My Car" (was this a reference to McCartney's accident?); "I'm Only Sleeping" (a reference to Paul in an unmarked grave?); "Nowhere Man" (perhaps a clue that McCartney was now a corpse?); "Dr. Robert" (though this song was written about a drug supplier it could have suggested the mysterious doctor who signed Paul's death certificate); "Yesterday" (the way the Beatles were before McCartney's tragic end); "Act Naturally" (the way the Beatles have gone on, pretending that Paul was still alive); "If I Needed Someone" (did the Beatles need a replacement for Paul to complete the band?); and "We Can Work It Out" (a reference to the Beatles and their management promoting the cover-up of Paul's death).

Today, the original *Yesterday And Today* LP with the "Butcher Cover" is a collector's item bringing prices in the thousands. Of course the cover must be carefully steamed away to reveal this hidden prize, perhaps suggesting another clue to encourage the public to examine each Beatle product carefully to find the truth. Besides, Lennon mentioned that the Beatles were bored and this gave them an excellent outlet to provide further clues to a tragic death, and didn't John once state that Americans would buy anything?

Parlophone re-released a collection of Beatle hits for the British market in December of 1966. This import is called *A Collection of Beatle Oldies* (Parlophone PMC7016:PCS7016). The album was released in Great Britain on December 10, 1966, which meant that it immediately preceded *Sgt. Pepper's* and may have included the first clues to the "Paul Is Dead" rumors.

The cover presents the Beatles in the upper left hand corner posing by a convertible. One of the figures, who resembles Paul to some degree, is holding a cigarette in his right hand (a clue that is later repeated on the *Abbey Road* cover). There is a large blowup of a Beatle figure sitting upon a bass drum which proclaims OLDIES in large capital letters. The drawing also pictures a car with its headlights on (representing a late night drive, or a drive perhaps occurring on a Wednesday morning at 5 o'clock) heading off the road in what appears to be a collision course with the large Beatle figures' head. Remember, the rumor suggested that Paul had died from decapitation or from a serious head injury. The larger-than-life figure is dressed in Mod clothing and the face is shadowed. It is odd that this is the only area that is shadowed on the entire body.

This could well suggest Robert Freeman's *With The Beatles* in which shadows play a dominant role in each Beatle's facial photograph. There is a strange coincidence concerning the placement of the shadowed face. The Beatle figure's head is in the upper right corner of the album jacket -- the exact location of Paul McCartney's photograph on the *With The Beatles* LP cover.

Since the bass drum provided such an incredible clue with *Sgt. Pepper's,* perhaps there would be another hidden message on the Oldies drumskin. Notice that the last four letters in "Oldies" is "dies." In an alphabetical sequence by raising the letters "O" and "L" one letter each we get the letters "P" and "M". When the phrase is read together it appears to suggest P (Paul) M (McCartney) Dies.

In the back cover photograph, Paul is the only Beatle dressed in black. To some, including my friend Chet from Texas, the large figure resting upon the bass drum may suggest McCartney's replacement, a replacement whose facial features resemble none of the actual members of the Beatles, but instead bears the features of a complete stranger. This may well be a stretch but it is a work of great imagination and it is still great fun searching for clues to a twenty-five-year-old mystery.

CHAPTER 4

The Impostor Theory:

*Let Me Introduce To You,
The One And Only Billy Shears.*

"Sergeant Pepper's Lonely
Hearts Club Band "

The *Revolver* LP was released in England on August 5, 1966, and in the United States on August 8, 1966. This album included "Got To Get You Into My Life" which featured the opening lyric: "I was alone. I took a ride. I didn't know what I would find there." Could this line have also referred to Paul's mysterious death? Surely not, since the Beatles were preparing to leave on the tour that later proved to be their last. To be significant to the car crash all clues must come after the Candlestick Park Concert. Obviously, some fans jumped at any clue that may have suggested the fatal crash or Paul's being alone and not knowing that he was very close to the hereafter.

The song "She Said She Said" contained a line: "I know what its like to be dead." In the *Playboy Interviews,* Lennon recalled that "She Said She Said" was "written after an acid trip in L.A. during a break in the Beatles' tour [August 1965] where we were having fun with the Byrds and lots of girls. . .Peter Fonda came in when we were on acid and he kept coming up to me and sitting next to me and whispering 'I know what its like to be dead.' He was describing an acid trip he had been on. We didn't want to hear about that! We were on an acid trip and the sun was shining and the girls were dancing and the whole thing was beautiful and sixties, and this guy -- who I really didn't know; he hadn't made *Easy Rider* or anything -- kept coming over, wearing shades, saying, 'I know what it's like to be dead,' and we kept leaving him because he was so boring! And I used it for the song, but I changed it to 'she' not 'he.' It was scary. You know, a guy. . .when you're flying high and [whispers] 'I know what it's like to be dead, man.' I remembered the incident. Don't tell me about it! I don't want to know what it's like to be dead" (Sheff, 160).

Devoted followers of the macabre decided that the gender change was only another attempt at keeping the tragedy from the public. The term "revolver" evoked images of change. Just as the cylinder turns in a handgun, or revolver, for the purpose of ejecting spent cartridges, so might the Beatles have moved to replace a fallen member with a new substitute. The album cover displayed McCartney's likeness in a profile suggesting that his picture was pieced into the drawing with the other members. No matter how absurd these clues sounded, the public had a heyday as they searched through old Beatle albums and read double meanings into every lyric line. No one will ever know for sure just how many turntables were ruined by overzealous fans who turned the platters backwards and destroyed the delicate mechanisms inside the players.

If the visual clues could be taken literally and Paul McCartney actually died in an automobile accident on November 9, 1966, then who was the mysterious Paul on the *Sgt. Pepper's* album cover? When the death rumors circulated throughout the press, fans and other sleuths formulated somewhat incredible theories about the identity of the impostor Beatle. Some sources claimed that the new Paul was an actor named William Campbell. Campbell was supposedly the winner of a Paul McCartney look-alike contest and conveniently, an orphan from Edinburgh. This replacement allegedly went as far as to have had plastic surgery to make the resemblance closer (Dowlding, 158). Of course it didn't hurt that Campbell could write the same types of songs as the real McCartney and just happened to have a voice that was also identical.

Under closer investigation researchers found a Campbelltown a few miles from Paul's home at Highgate. Perhaps this suggested another clue to the impostor's identity. However, a number of sleuths reasoned that if an impostor had taken McCartney's place then that must have supplied the motive that stopped the Beatles' live performances. It would have taken a great deal of time for the stand-in to have counterfeited the true Paul's performance. Besides, the public might have become aware of this cover-up when they attended the newly-scheduled Beatle concerts. Some overzealous fans noticed a strange picture of McCartney in disguise pasted on the liner sheet from *The White Album*. These fans were convinced that the Beatles were brazen enough to have actually printed a photograph of the look-alike in his natural appearance.

One interesting theory dealt with the true identity of the man in the blue band uniform on the back of *Sgt. Pepper's*. Though some Beatle insiders claimed that it was actually McCartney in the poses, *The Long and Winding Road: A History of the Beatles on Record* suggested that the mysterious Paul was Mal Evans, a Beatle road manager. It seemed that McCartney had made plans to be with his girlfriend, Jane Asher, in the United States to help celebrate her twenty-first birthday. Since Paul was unavailable for the photo sessions, Evans took his place but with his back facing the camera. In this case, there was evidence to support the supposition of an Beatle impostor. Of course, many observers noticed that there were photos of McCartney in a similar pose with his back to the camera. Believers in the conspiracy theory were convinced that the double was forced to turn his back to the camera to hide the freshly-healing scars from plastic surgery. Imagine their excitement when they noticed the scar above Paul's lip in the "Paperback Writer" video and on Paul's individual photo from *The White Album.* It seems that this may well remain one of the small mysteries of the *Sgt. Pepper's* sessions as to the actual identity of McCartney's double.

As the lines of *Sgt. Pepper's* title song rang out through our stereo speakers, we heard the singer [Paul McCartney] declare: "I don't really want to stop the show, but I thought that you might like to know, that the singer's going to sing a song, and he wants you all to sing along. So let me introduce to you, the one and only Billy Shears and Sgt. Pepper's Lonely Hearts Club Band." Why did Paul McCartney not want to stop the show? Did this mean that with the death of the popular Beatle, the road to riches and further glory would then be over for the three remaining group members, as well as for their record companies, publishing companies, and management? Does McCartney actually go as far as to introduce his double? Who was this mysterious Billy Shears?

One of the most fascinating rumors of this period dealt with a mysterious Beatle look-alike contest in the early sixties. The Paul McCartney look-alike winner's photograph was never published, but the rumor spread that his name was released as Billy Shears. "Billy Shears" could well have been a pseudonym for William Campbell. McCartney mentioned that the Beatles used the name Billy Shears only for its "poetic ring" (Dowlding, 165). Death clue advocates then proposed that this was the Beatles' first introduction of the substitute. Lee Merrick wrote an article for *The Rat Subterranean News* which suggested the Billy Shears impostor theory on October 29, 1969. Merrick also stated the impostor's father was Philip Shears who lived in Chelsea.

When the first song, "Sgt. Pepper's," faded into the next composition, "With a Little Help From My Friends," the listener heard the band sing "B-I-L-L-Y S-H-E-A-R-S." When Ringo sang the first line to this number his first phrase was "What would you think if I sang out of tune, would you stand up and walk out on me? Lend me your ears and I'll sing you a song, and I'll try not to sing out of key." Why would one of the Beatles have to worry about singing out of key? Was this reference to a hidden insecurity that the public would not accept a replacement in the popular group?

Upon closer listening, it sounded almost like an apology to the audience. The chorus stated that the singer would "get by with a little help from my friends. . .I get high with a little help from my friends. . .going to try with a little help from my friends." The lines "get high with a little help from my friends" became a highly-debated topic in 1970. Then Vice President Spiro Agnew actually led a grass roots campaign to remove this drug-related song from American airways. This attempt failed. Obviously, Mr. Agnew suspected that these obscure "friends" must be directly related to the same family members that the Rolling Stones alluded to as "little yellow pills" in their song "Mother's Little Helper." In both works, the title characters managed to "get by." The Beatles steadfastly denied that their composition had anything to do with drug use. It was almost too coincidental that the Beatles next song was entitled "Lucy In The Sky With Diamonds." The Carrollian symbols of "marmalade skies" and "kaleidoscope eyes" took the listener into a surrealistic dream world of colorful images. It didn't take the hip generation long to grasp the hidden meaning in the title; "Lucy," "Sky," and "Diamonds" served as an acronym for LSD.

Lennon, in the *Playboy Interviews,* related: "My son Julian came in one day with a picture he painted about a school friend named Lucy. He had sketched in some stars in the sky and called it 'Lucy in The Sky with Diamonds.' Simple."

Beatle aide Pete Shotton also remembered: "I also happened to be there the day Julian came home from school with a pastel drawing of his classmate Lucy's face against a backdrop of exploding multicolored stars. Unusually impressed with his son's handiwork, John asked what the drawing was called. 'It's Lucy in the Sky With Diamonds, Daddy,' Julian replied. . .though John was certainly ingesting inordinate amounts of acid around the time he wrote 'Lucy in the Sky With Diamonds,' the pun was indeed sheer coincidence" (Dowlding, 166).

Lennon maintained his interpretation of "Lucy" throughout his life. He commented, "'Lucy In The Sky With Diamonds' -- I swear to God or Mao, or to anybody you like, I had no idea spelled LSD -- I didn't look at the initials, I don't look -- I mean, I never play things backward" (*Rolling Stone*, February 4, 1971).

Drug references denied, it seemed likely that another avenue of meaning had to be explored. If the "friends" were not drugs, then what could they be? Maybe the clue was suggested in the last line, "I get by with a little help from my friends." Perhaps this line referred to the cover-up in which the impostor maintained his hidden existence only through the help of his friends -- in this case the Beatles and their management. This seemed a distinct possibility, or at least sounded plausible. Perhaps this was only another piece of the puzzle that had become one of the greatest mysteries in music history.

Sgt. Pepper's was recognized as "a new and golden renaissance of song" by *The New York Review of Books*. Timothy Leary, LSD apostle, described the album: "The *Sgt. Pepper's* album. . .compresses the evolutionary development of musicology and much of the history of Eastern and Western sound in a new tympanic complexity. The Beatles are Divine Messiahs. Prototypes of a new young race of laughing free men" (Dowlding, 162).

It seemed that the world had ironically taken Dr. Leary's famous suggestion to "Turn on, Tune In, And Drop Out." David Crosby of the Byrds and later of Crosby, Stills, Nash, and Young fame stated: "Somehow *Sgt. Pepper's* did not stop the Vietnam War. Somehow it didn't work. Somebody isn't listening. . .I would've thought *Sgt. Pepper's* could've stopped the war just by putting too many good vibes in the air for anybody to have a war around" (Dowlding, 163).

But all was not lost. True, another illusion of life was shaken by the premise that mankind was still not ready for peace and harmony, but *Sgt. Pepper's* did manage to stand as the greatest rock album of all time as voted by critics and broadcasters in Paul Gambaccini's *The Top 100 Rock and Roll Albums of all Time*, an award the album won both in the 1977 and 1987 editions.

Sgt. Pepper's Lonely Hearts Club Band also illustrated that the Beatles maintained a sense of humor. At the conclusion of the recording, a

----

high-frequency note at about 18 kilocycles per second was originally added to the run-out groove on the second side of the album. It is inaudible to humans, but dogs can hear it. A few seconds of gibberish were included on the run-out groove. McCartney suggested it for the benefit of people who had a turntable that didn't shut off. The needle would go around and around in the groove without shutting off, and some gibberish in that groove was deemed better than hiss. Listeners stated that the gibberish said, "Lucy Abbey all the way" or "He's found Heaven." When the tape is reversed, a voice is said to say, "We'll all be back here soon." This could well be a Freudian nightmare!

When Paul McCartney talked to journalist Paul Gambaccini in December, 1973, he told this story about the hidden meaning: "I went inside. . .and played it studiously, turned it backwards with my thumb against the motor, turned the motor off and did it backwards. And there it was, plain as anything, "We'll f**k you like Supermen." I thought, Jesus, what can you do?" (*Rolling Stone* No. 153, January 31, 1974/ Hockinson, 99).

Recording the two seconds of gibberish took a full night, from 7 PM to 3 AM, more than half the time it took to record the Beatles' entire first album (Dowlding, 160). Recording engineer Geoff Emerick, and producer George Martin calculated that the *Sgt. Pepper's* LP took a total of 700 hours to complete, whereas the Beatles' first album, *Please Please Me*, took a grand total of 585 minutes.

CHAPTER 5

The Mystery of the Magical Mystery Tour

What? Is He Dead?/
Goo Goo Goo Joob

"I Am the Walrus"

The search for more clues to the untimely demise of Paul McCartney continued with the release of *Magical Mystery Tour* on December 8, 1967, in Great Britain as a soundtrack to the Beatle film of the same title. *Magical Mystery Tour* included a twenty-four page booklet of stills from the film. The United States release was on November 27, 1967, and included Beatles singles from 1967 like "Hello Goodbye." Some of the new songs were actually written for the *Sgt. Pepper's* album .("Strawberry Fields Forever") and placed on the album as an afterthought.

Magical Mystery Tour, the British television film, made its debut on December 26. British critics had a field day with their abuse. Such phrases as "The harder they come, the harder they fall"; "I cannot ever remember seeing such blatant rubbish"; "chaotic"; "appalling"; and "a colossal conceit" (Schaffner, 90) greeted the Beatles in the morning papers following the preview. Now it seemed that the Beatles were fallible. They had fallen from grace.

Paul McCartney blamed the film's failure on the BBC's decision to broadcast the film in black and white. The Beatle interest preferred the original color version to the drab black and white version. It seemed that the most reasonable explanation for this unexpected failure by the Beatles was the reported drug overdose of manager Brian Epstein on August 27, 1967. He died at the age of thirty-two. Epstein had been the glue that held the now discordant bonds together. Without him, the group was adrift and headed for destruction. Beatle fans, however, plodded steadily along in their quest for the truth. What new death clues did this LP hold?

The title song "Magical Mystery Tour" advised us to "roll up for the mystery tour." What was the mystery? We found that the last line, "The magical mystery tour is dying to take you away. Dying to take you away -- take you today" suggested again that the mystery concerned death. Perhaps the mystery contained more answers to the supposed death of McCartney, and the tour would be a presentation of those clues.

The album jacket contained a photograph of the Beatles dressed in animal costumes. In the center was a black walrus. In certain Scandinavian countries, a walrus is considered a harbinger of death. Immediately, researchers speculated that the McCartney impostor was dressed in the walrus skins.

In *The Beatles Forever,* author Nicholas Schaffner cited that the term "walrus" was derived from Greek and meant "corpse." Of course *Webster's Dictionary* lists that the term "walrus" is from Scandinavian origin, but certainly does not mean corpse. With this in mind, the public latched on to another clue. It didn't really matter that John Lennon actually claimed that it was he dressed in the walrus costume, because upon closer examination of the song title, the answer became more evident. The complete title is "I Am The Walrus ('No You're Not!' Said Little Nicola)." Lennon claimed to be the walrus when we are told explicitly that he is not. If Lennon was not the corpse, then who was?

In a later Beatle album release, *The White Album,* Lennon chose to reveal the identity of the supposed corpse in the song "Glass Onion." In the second verse, Lennon sang: "I told you 'bout the walrus and me, man, you know that we're as close as can be man. Well here's another clue for you all. . .the walrus was Paul." This marked the first time that the walrus symbol was associated with any member of the Beatles except for Lennon's claim that he was the walrus.

Also on the album cover was a bird-like creature standing over the left shoulder of the black walrus. This bird-like animal wore John's trademark gold-rimmed glasses, thus providing another clue that John certainly was not the walrus!

One of the strangest clues from *Magical Mystery Tour* concerned Ringo's drumhead. The drum skin reads "Love the 3 Beatles." Does this suggest that there were only three Beatles left to love? Notice that on pages 10 and 13 of the tour booklet, Paul is standing barefoot in his socks. This, like the *Abbey Road* cover, suggested that in some countries, corpses are buried without their shoes. If you look to the left of Ringo's

---

bass drum, you can see Paul's empty shoes -- smeared with what appears to be blood.

David Sheff's *The Playboy Interviews with John Lennon and Yoko Ono* contained the following dialogue with John Lennon:

Playboy: "The most obvious [misinterpretation of Beatle lyrics] is the 'Paul Is Dead' thing. . .what about 'here's another clue for you all, the walrus was Paul' from 'Glass Onion'?"

Lennon: "Well, that was a joke. The line was put in partly because I was feeling guilty because I was with Yoko and I was leaving Paul. I was trying -- I don't know. It's a very perverse way of saying to Paul, you know, 'Here, have this crumb, this illusion, this -- this stroke, because I'm leaving'" (Sheff, 78).

Later in the same interview, Lennon made an additional comment about "Glass Onion":

Lennon: "That's me, just doing a throwaway song, a la 'Walrus,' a la everything I've ever written. I threw the line in -- 'The Walrus Was Paul' -- just to confuse everybody a bit more. And I thought 'Walrus' has now become me, meaning 'I am the one.' Only it didn't mean that in this song."

Playboy: "Why a Walrus?"

Lennon: "It could've been 'The fox terrier is Paul,' you know. I mean, it's just a bit of poetry. It was just thrown in like that" (Sheff, 177).

According to these comments, Lennon had accomplished his goal: now, we were all confused!

The Beatles had long been known for their sense of humor. In the 1965 Beatle classic "Girl," the Beatles produced a back-up harmony line that stated "tit tit tit". Other examples of Beatle humor included the Butcher album cover, the end grooves of "Sgt. Pepper's" (the high frequency dog whistle and the never ending fade out loop), and a supposed reference to Brian Epstein's sexual preferences in "Baby You're A Rich Man." The group was suspected of singing, "Baby you're a rich fag Jew," along with the lyric, "Baby you're a rich man too."

At times in their careers, the Fab Four had been accused of bigotry and anti-Semitism. In a bootleg recording of "Get Back" Paul

McCartney was accused of singing: "Siddiatawher was a Pakistani living in another land, always heard it all around. Don't dig no Pakistanis taking all the people's jobs." The reference to 'Pakistanis' had to deal with the immigration of Pakistani citizens to England in 1969 (Dowlding, 267).

McCartney's reply to his apparent racial overtones was made in the September 11, 1986, edition of *Rolling Stone.*

According to McCartney: "When we were doing *Let It Be,* there were a couple of verses to 'Get Back' which were actually not racist at all -- they were anti-racist. There were a lot of stories in the newspapers then about Pakistanis crowding out flats -- you know, living sixteen to a room or whatever. So in one of the verses of 'Get Back', which we were making up on the set of *Let It Be* [the film], one of the out takes has something about 'too many Pakistanis living in a council flat' -- that's the line. Which to me was actually talking out against overcrowding for Pakistanis. If there was any group that was not racist, it was the Beatles. I mean, all our favorite people were always black. We were kind of the first people to open international eyes, in a way, to Motown."

McCartney was correct according to Dowlding: "The Beatles made at least two public gestures against racism: they consented to perform on September 11, 1964, in Jacksonville, Alabama, only after promoters agreed to admit nonwhites to the show, and on July 29, 1966, they refused to sign a contract for a series of concerts in South Africa" (Dowlding, 268). With this concern it would be hard to consider the Beatles racist. It is evident that none of their released recordings even hint at racism. Instead, the Beatles lyrically longed for a world of peaceful coexistence with complete equality for all.

The track "I Am The Walrus" still contained more examples of strange clues and bizarre symbols. As previously mentioned, Lennon was greatly influenced by Lewis Carroll and even received his inspiration for the song from Carroll's "The Walrus And The Carpenter." According to Lennon, "The first line [to 'I Am The Walrus'] was written on one acid trip one weekend, the second line on another acid trip the next weekend, and it was filled in after I met Yoko. . .it's from 'The Walrus And The Carpenter.' *Alice In Wonderland.* To me, it was a beautiful poem. It never dawned on me that Lewis Carroll was commenting on the capitalist system. I never went into that bit about what he really meant, like people are doing with the Beatles' work. Later, I went back and looked at it and realized that the walrus was the bad guy in the story and the carpenter was the good guy. I thought, 'Oh, shit, I picked the wrong guy. I should have said, 'I am the carpenter.' But that wouldn't have been the same, would it?" (Sheff, 164).

As far as being the same, Lennon was probably right. If the song had been entitled "I Am The Carpenter," the religious right would have sworn that Lennon had compared himself to Christ. Surely, John was not ready to start another zealous religious inquisition against himself. . .or was he? On the other hand, Lennon may well have put a great deal of thought into his title. Perhaps he was the walrus.

In the poem, the walrus tricks a group of oysters into taking a walk along the beach. The oysters become the victims of the walrus's cruel hoax. Was John Lennon making the public his gullible oysters?

One of the most intriguing lyrics in "I Am The Walrus" is the repeated phrase "Goo goo goo joob." This phrase, supposedly taken from James Joyce's *Finnegan's Wake,* were the last words spoken by Humpty Dumpty before his famous fall. In a way, it is most appropriate for Humpty Dumpty to be introduced here. Like the "Paul Is Dead" theory, Humpty Dumpty also had a tragic accident and cracked his head.

In Lewis Carroll's *Through The Looking Glass,* Humpty Dumpty answers Alice's question, "Must a name mean something?" to which the eggman replies, "Of course it must!"

The work presents a series of riddles as Humpty Dumpty attempts to interpret the meaning to Carroll's "Jabberwocky." These references to "Jabberwocky" hint at the same Carollian word play that Lennon enjoyed through his abstract lyrics. These riddles could have inspired Lennon to try the ultimate challenge -- placing visual and audio clues that dealt with the mysterious death of one of the Beatles. Lewis Carroll would have been proud!

Lennon and McCartney must have had a great laugh at all the interpretations to the given clues, a scene which brings to mind Humpty Dumpty's fractured translation of "Jabberwocky" and reinforced Humpty's thought: "I can explain all the poems that ever were invented -- and a good many that haven't been invented yet." Perhaps Humpty Dumpty's interpretations fit perfectly with Lennon's attempt to baffle and confuse the intellectuals who insisted that each Beatles lyric had a complex and hidden meaning.

The archetypal fall can be interpreted in a number of ways. First, the fall could have suggested the fall of the Beatles themselves as a group.

The group was no longer the darling of the media. They had been savagely attacked by the critics for their failure in the *Magical Mystery Tour* film. Organized religion perceived the Beatles as a threat of corruption to the morals of American youth. Spiro Agnew had led the unsuccessful campaign to remove tainted drug-induced Beatle songs from the American airways. It remained to be seen if the Fab Four would become Milton's Satan and lose Paradise forever. Was it better "to reign in Hell than serve in Heaven"? Could the Beatles give up the adoring fans and reveal their true, yet somewhat unpopular political leanings -- opposing the Vietnam War -- and divulge their acceptance of the drug culture? The group could follow in the footsteps of Socrates, who also was accused of corrupting the youth of his era, and become the sacrificial scapegoats of social inflexibility.

Secondly, the fall could relate to McCartney's supposed accident. Like Humpty Dumpty's topple off the wall, Paul's accident could bear similarity in that "all the king's horses and all the king's men" -- in this instance the remaining members, the record companies, the production and management firms, and the adoring public -- could not bring the real Paul back from the shadowy realms of the dead. The missing pieces would have to be haphazardly rearranged as a make-shift replacement. This replacement would imitate the true McCartney, in turn keeping the financial empire solvent. It just depended on whether they wanted to play pass the hemlock!

Lastly, the archetypal fall might have suggested the first clues that the Beatles were on their way to a break-up. As Humpty Dumpty fell and broke into the small fragments that could never again be joined together, perhaps the Beatles, either knowingly or subconsciously, were experiencing their own death throes.

During the making of *Rubber Soul,* tensions between the Beatles grew. Chris Salewicz's *McCartney* cites the following comment from Norman Smith: "With *Rubber Soul,* the clash between John and Paul was becoming obvious. Also, George was having to put up with an awful lot from Paul. We now had the luxury of four-track recording, so George would put his solo on afterward. But as far as Paul concerned, George could do no right -- Paul was absolutely finicky. So what would happen was that on certain songs Paul himself played the solos. I would wonder what the hell was going on, because George would have done two or three takes, and to me they were really quite okay. But Paul would be saying,

'No, no, no!' And he'd start quoting American records, telling him to play exactly as he'd heard on such-and-such a song. So we'd go back from the top, and George would really get into it. Then would come Paul's comment, 'Okay, the first sixteen bars weren't bad, but that middle.' Then Paul would take over and do it himself -- he always had a left-handed guitar with him. Subsequently, I discovered that George Harrison had been hating Paul's bloody guts for this, but it didn't show itself. . .mind you, there is no doubt at all that Paul was the main musical force. . .also in terms of production as well. A lot of the time George Martin didn't really have to do the things he did because Paul McCartney was around and could have done them equally well. The only thing he couldn't do was to put symbols to chords; he couldn't write music. But he could most certainly tell an arranger how to do it, just by singing a part -- however, he didn't know, of course, whether the strings or brass could play what he wanted. But most of the ideas came from Paul."

On the *Sgt. Pepper's* cover we observed the Beatles dressed in brightly colored band uniforms. Each uniform was unique and entirely different vibrant colors. Could this have suggested that the group now considered themselves solely as individuals and not as the similarly clad mop tops from 1964? Perhaps this is why the wax figures are shown gazing down upon a grave. A grave with "Beatles" neatly arranged in a floral funeral setting combined the ending of one era with the promising, but also a fatalistic, rebirth of a new order.

The Humpty Dumpty clues proved rather interesting, but the first line of "I Am The Walrus" contained a somewhat sinister reference. The lyric stated: "I am he as you are he as you are me and we are all together." This confusing word play reference contained Carrollian influences. Lennon had created his own "Jabberwocky" with what appeared to be words that were related only through nonsense. But what if the phrase was interpreted to mean that the unknown "he" was actually Paul McCartney? How could Lennon have possibly been McCartney? And if the mysterious "you" refers to the other Beatles [George and Ringo] how could they also have managed to take the place of their fallen fellow musician and business partner? What if the lines merely suggested that the remaining Beatles would take the place of McCartney in the recording studio. Lennon and Harrison could have played his bass parts; John Lennon could have easily covered the vocals since it was he who sang most of the Beatle songs.

The November 7, 1969, issue of *Life* magazine presented a picture of two sonograms taken by a Dr. Henry M. Truby of the University of Miami. The sonogram of McCartney singing a phrase from "Hey Jude" was suspiciously different from the sonogram containing the phrase "all my troubles" from the earlier recording of "Yesterday." The results? The voices did not match. Could this suggest that there could have been more than one McCartney? Actually, Truby's study stated that there may have been three McCartneys.

Some experts suggested that the sonograms in question were a closer match to John Lennon. This possible cover-up paralleled the lyric from "A Little Help From My Friends." In this case, the Beatles had managed to get by with a little help from their friends. The recordings were made by the band, while the impostor only had to stand and pretend to perform in the Beatle-made films. Incidentally, the BBC banned the promotional film of "Hello Goodbye" because McCartney was lip-syncing his vocal. This violated the rules of the British musicians' union (Dowlding, 190). Obviously, Milli Vanilli was not the first!

"Hello Goodbye" also hinted at a beginning from an end. Could this have been the McCartney imitator who sang, "I don't know why you say goodbye, I say hello?" This might have served as a lyrical clue sang by the mysterious replacement, William Campbell, who luckily stumbled into the role of a lifetime. All he had to do was resemble McCartney, keep the terrible secret, and collect his share of the huge sums of money from the Beatle royalties.

James Joyce's *Finnegan's Wake* also suggested other macabre parallels to the impostor theories. The main character, Tim Finnegan, became drunk and fell from a ladder. Everyone thought that he died from the fall and his friends held a wake around his body to commemorate his passing. The wake turned into a drunken party ("mirth in funeral") and one of the revelers accidentally poured whisky upon the corpse. Finnegan arose from his coffin and joined in the party. The members of the wake, however, held Tim in his coffin and informed him that an impostor was due to take his place. This impostor, Humphrey Chimpden Earwicker, assumed the role of the good Tim Finnegan. The impostor's initials, H.C.E., was used variously as "Here Comes Everybody." Lennon surely enjoyed such word play. The mysterious H.C.E. was said to have suffered from an obscure disease, perhaps venereal, and peeped at or exposed himself to girls in Phoenix Park. This section of *Finnegan's Wake* strongly

----

resembled Lennon's lines from "I Am The Walrus": "Crabalocker fishwife pornographic priestess boy, you been a naughty girl, you let your knickers down." In this phrase we see Lennon's word play along with the parallel to Earwicker's exhibitionist feats at Phoenix Park.

Joseph Campbell and Henry Morton Robinson's *A Skeleton Key To Finnegan's Wake* suggested: "[Tim Finnegan] is symbolic of Finn McCall, captain for two hundred years of Ireland's warrior-heroes and most famous of Dublin's early giants -- Finn is an archetype for all heroes, Thor, Prometheus, Osirius, Christ, and Buddha -- in whose life and through whose inspiration the race lives. It is Finn's coming again (Finn-again) that strength and hope are provided for man-kind" (Campbell and Robinson, 4).

John Lennon presents further references to Humpty Dumpty throughout "I Am The Walrus" by the Beatles becoming the "eggmen" who represented the cosmic egg of creation itself. The egg symbolically represented "potentiality, the seed of generation, the mystery of life" (Cirlot, 94). The Egyptians believed that the egg contained all that was hidden from mortal man in life, including the occult. "In the Egyptian Ritual, the universe is termed the 'egg conceived in the hour of the Great One of the dual force.' The god Ra is displayed resplendent in his egg. An illustration on a papyrus, in the *Edipus AEgypticus of Kircher* (III, 124) shows the image of an egg floating above a mummy, signifying hope of life hereafter" (Cirlot, 94). This reference to the "eggman" may have represented the cosmic rebirth of the Beatle essence and evolution of spirit to an ideal state of wisdom and love.

In *The Lives of John Lennon*, author Albert Goldman states that the mysterious "eggman" was John's nickname for Eric Burdon, lead singer for the Animals. According to Goldman, Burdon was "notorious for cracking eggs on the naked bodies of girls to whom he was making love" (Goldman, 286).

Joyce referred graphically to the members of the wake, the watchers, as they ate everything including Finnegan's body of which Campbell and Robinson related to the Eucharist: "The cosmic egg is shattered but the egg substance is gathered and served for the nutriment of the people, 'sunny side up with care'" (Campbell and Robinson, 5).

The archetypal fall of Humpty Dumpty, the "egg man," relates to this cosmic and metaphysical rebirth. Perhaps the fall is likened to the fall of Adam and man's redemption from original sin, with the end result being the resurrection of hope and the obtaining of the ideal worlds of wisdom and love with the final defeat and destruction of ignorance and intolerance.

Other passages from *Finnegan's Wake* made a case for the elaborate theory of Paul's death. On the *Sgt. Pepper's* album's front cover, the crowd could have been an allusion to the wake. The hand above McCartney's head may have been a symbolic reference to Finnegan's being held in the coffin, or in this case, the decorated grave.

Other lines from the lyric provided further clues to McCartney's tragic doom. Lennon mentioned a "stupid bloody Tuesday" which may have alluded to the night McCartney left Abbey Road studios. Although the fatal accident occurred on a Wednesday morning at 5 AM, McCartney supposedly left the studio earlier in the night due to an argument, which would have provided him plenty of time for his rendezvous with destiny.

Lennon also mentioned the phrase "waiting for the van to come," which may have been reference to the parked van that was involved in the fatal crash of Tara Browne, the Guinness heir, and an allusion to the accident scene in "A Day In The Life."

Possibly the most fascinating section of "I Am The Walrus" dealt with the obscure hidden references in the song's long fade-out. Mixed voices that chant "oom pah, oom pah, stick it up your jumpah," and "everybody's got one, everybody's got one" along with the droning "goo goo goo joob" are mixed with a frantic orchestral score with cellos and violins ascending and descending in chaotic disorder. Some listeners claim that if the track is reversed the "everybody's got one" becomes "Paul Is Dead, ha, ha," but again, this could be another incredible stretch.

At the conclusion, just before the fade out, actors recite passages from Shakespeare's *King Lear* (4.6.250-60):

Oswald: "Slave, thou hast slain me. Villain, take my purse. If ever thou wilt thrive, BURY MY BODY, and give the letters which thou find'st about me to Edmund Earl of Gloucester. Seek him out upon the British party. OH, UNTIMELY DEATH!"

Edgar: "I know thee well -- a serviceable villain, as duteous to the vices of thy mistress as badness would desire."

Gloucester: "WHAT, IS HE DEAD?"

Edgar: "Sit you down, Father, rest you."

It is interesting that Lennon chose these lines by accident. According to Lennon, "There was some live BBC radio on one track, y'know. They were reciting Shakespeare or something and I just fed whatever lines were on the radio right into the song" (Sheff, 164).

King Lear, considered by many critics to be Shakespeare's masterpiece, is a tale of a foolish king who unwisely divided his kingdom between his daughters based on his concept of their love for him. Tragically, he found that Cordelia, the youngest daughter, was the most devoted and loved her father through a child's natural duty and not by exaggerated pretense for gain.

King Lear, however, was a play within a play and the other story line bore the strongest significance to the quoted lines. The Earl of Gloucester, like Lear, rushed to judgment and for this rash mistake, suffered greatly. The Earl of Gloucester's crime was being tricked by an impostor. Gloucester's illegitimate son, Edmund, determined to take the inheritance of his half brother, Edgar, accomplishes this task by interchanging letters. These false letters led to Edgar's disinheritance and these hidden secrets related to the outcome of the tragic conflicts.

The actors' lines bore a striking resemblance to the McCartney mystery. For example, "Slave, thou hast slain me. Villain take my purse" may relate to an impostor taking Paul's place following his tragic death. The goal simply being for corporate financial gain. Other bizarre phrases included: "bury my body," "oh, untimely death," and "what, is he dead?" Adding these lines of dialogue seemed almost too pertinent to the mystery -- something far more than a simple mistake or mere coincidence. Besides, there is another reference to *Lear* in the earlier Beatle song "Paperback Writer": "Dear sir or madam won't you read my book. It took me years to write. Won't you take a look? It's based on a novel by a man named Lear and I need a break and I wanna be a paperback writer." This substantiated that Lennon and McCartney were well studied in the tragedy of *King Lear.*

The Magical Mystery Tour contained other evidence to the fatal end of McCartney. As sleuths pored through the song booklet, careful observers noticed photographs of Paul as cast members posed with their hands raised above the Beatle's head -- a death clue reference that would be repeated in the Beatles' motion picture *Yellow Submarine.* In one still from *The Magical Mystery Tour,* McCartney sits at a desk behind a sign stating "I Was." The British flags behind Paul are crossed in the same pattern used for military funerals. McCartney, of course, is dressed appropriately in a military uniform.

In another still from *Magical Mystery Tour*, the Beatles are dressed in white evening clothes. While John, George, and Ringo wear red carnations in their lapels, McCartney wears a black carnation. Again, McCartney stands out from the others. The black flower was interpreted as a death symbol. In the film production, the Beatles descended a spiral staircase while "Your Mother Should Know" played in the background. McCartney later stated that "I was wearing a black flower because they [the film production crew] ran out of red ones." How lucky that an ordinary black carnation should be backstage! Some investigators insist that if you look closely, the carnations are actually painted upon the Beatles' lapels. If this is true, the someone very close to the film's production made a calculated decision to create the flower mystery.

In this very scene, a young girl hands McCartney a bouquet of dead flowers. One of the most heavily-debated clues was found in *Magical Mystery Tour's* "Strawberry Fields Forever." Lennon stated: "Strawberry Fields is a Salvation Army home that was near the house I lived in with my auntie in the suburbs. There were two famous houses there. One was owned by Gladstone, which was a reformatory for boys, which I could see out my window. And Strawberry Fields was just around the corner from that. It was an old Victorian house converted for Salvation Army orphans, and as a kid I used to go to their garden parties with my friends. We'd go there and hang out and sell lemonade bottles for a penny and we always had fun at Strawberry Fields. Apparently, it used to be a farm that made strawberries or whatever. I don't know. But I just took the name -- it had nothing to do with the Salvation Army" (Sheff, 138).

The audible clue was found near the end of the recording, and came immediately after the music softly faded out only to slowly reemerge and build once more. Upon careful listening, a faint voice stated something like, "I buried Paul." And thus began the controversy.

David Sheff broached this subject in *Playboy Interviews*.

Sheff: "What about the line in 'I Am The Walrus' [sic]: 'I buried Paul'?"

Lennon: "I said, 'Cranberry sauce.' Cranberry sauce is all I said."

The puzzling, unanswered question was that the line did not come from "I Am The Walrus." Actually, the line was from "Strawberry Fields Forever." It seemed unbelievable that Lennon would have mistaken the location of such a controversial lyric.

In *The Beatles In Their Own Words*, Paul McCartney remembered: "That wasn't 'I buried Paul' at all, that was John saying 'cranberry sauce'...that's John's humor. John would say something totally out of sync, like 'cranberry sauce.' If you don't realize that John's apt to say 'cranberry sauce' when he feels like it, then you start to hear a funny little word there, and you think, aha!" (Dowlding, 150).

Lennon also stuck by his original interpretation in a *Rolling Stone* interview. However, Derek Taylor, one of the Beatles' agents, offered another explanation in a *Life* magazine feature entitled "The Magical McCartney Mystery": "He [Taylor] released a statement from Paul. He [Paul] was, Taylor said, off in the country with his family...as for the voice in 'Strawberry Fields,' claims Taylor, it is saying, 'I'm very bored' not 'I buried Paul.' That was as far as Taylor would go. The Beatles didn't expect people to go around reversing their records. He did admit that putting stuff in there in reverse was just the sort of something that sly John Lennon might have done."

It now seemed incredible that both Lennon and McCartney agreed on the hidden message while Derek Taylor heard a completely different message. The only thing on which all three agreed was that the eerie soft-spoken voice did not state "I buried Paul."

John Lennon did manage to spell out his own first name in Morse code. This can be found after Lennon sings: "Let me take you down 'cause I'm going to." At this point, in dots and dashes one can discern J-O-H-N. Obviously this was an attempt by Lennon to lay claim that this was his song -- not just another Lennon and McCartney composition.

If John Lennon had taken the time to place his own name in a cryptic code, then perhaps a number of the hidden messages concerning the "Paul Is Dead" rumors may not be as far-fetched as we once thought. Obviously, the Beatles enjoyed throwing in hidden bits of information to tease their fans. It is amazing that twenty-six years later, most fans are just now becoming aware of the Beatles' incredible senses of humor, and can perhaps listen to Beatle classics with a new regard.

Naturally, some fans wanted to find more exotic clues. If the tape is reversed at the beginning of George Harrison's "Blue Jay Way," a phonetic reversal seems to state "Paul is bloody, Paul is very bloody." This section is the reverse of "Please don't be long, please don't you be very long" and again, this may well be a case of the listener hearing what he or she wants to hear. Actually, George was waiting for his good friend Derek Taylor in a rented house on Blue Jay Way in Los Angeles. If you can hear this hidden message, it may represent the first true phonetic reversal by the Beatles, coming much earlier than *The White Album's* "Revolution 9."

Another rumor circulating at the time stated that if the sleuth turned the album jacket upside down and looked at the *Magical Mystery Tour* album jacket's reflection in a mirror, another similarity to *Through The Looking Glass*, the title, detailed as stars, became the digits to a phone number upon reversal. The rumor further explained that if the number were dialed, the listener would get the true details of Paul McCartney's death.

In *Shout: The Beatles In Their Generation*, Philip Norman shares this information: "It was said that by holding *The Magical Mystery Tour's* EP sleeve up to a mirror, a telephone number became visible on which Paul himself could be contacted in the hereafter. The number in fact belonged to a Guardian journalist, subsequently driven almost to dementia by hundreds of early morning transatlantic telephone calls" (Norman, 387).

Theorists determined that in order to properly see the hidden phone number, the large yellow stars in "BEATLES" must be connected and then reversed in a mirror. Supposedly, there are three numbers depending on whether the album jacket is upside down or not. Besides the angry Guardian journalist, some listeners heard a voice stating "You're getting closer." Others swear that the phone number belonged to a funeral home while others claim that a voice belonging to Billy Shears quizzed them on Beatle trivia. Perhaps the callers should have made their calls on Wednesday morning at five o'clock.

Many believed the mysterious M&D company, scrawled on the chalkboard that John Lennon stands next to in *The Magical Mystery Tour* booklet, may be a funeral parlor. Many followers of the ironic correctly point out that the caption in question states "The best way to go is by M&D Company." M, D, and C form the initials of Lennon's murderer Mark David Chapman. This irony, however, tends to be much too disturbing.

CHAPTER 6

The White Album

Here's Another Clue For You All
-- The Walrus Was Paul!

"Glass Onion"

For the first time in their careers, the Beatles were convinced that the timing was right to release a double album. This double album represented Paul and John separately, as individuals who performed their songs with the other members filling the roles of back-up musicians. Obviously, it was a turbulent time.

The Beatles were disintegrating slowly and tension filled the studio sound rooms. In a *Musician* magazine interview dated February, 1985, Paul McCartney stated: "*The White Album* was the tension album. We were all in the midst of the psychedelic thing, or just coming out of it. In any case, it was weird. Never before had we recorded with beds in the studio. . .[Reportedly, Yoko Ono moved her bed into the studio during the recording sessions and even followed John into the men's rest room]. . .and people visiting for hours on end; business meetings and all that. There was a lot of friction. It was the weirdest experience because we were about to break up, that was tense in itself" (Dowlding, 219).

George Harrison commented, "Paul would always help along when you'd done his ten songs -- then when he got 'round to doing one of my songs, he would help. It was silly. It was very selfish, actually" (Dowlding, 218).

Most of this tension was instigated by John Lennon's intense love affair with Yoko Ono. In his biography entitled *Lennon*, Ray Coleman revealed that the other Beatles treated Yoko terribly: "John broke a rigid, unwritten rule of the group: that their women would never be allowed in the studios. John perversely attended every session for *The White Album* with Yoko by his side. His message, unspoken, was obvious to all: they were inseparable. She sat on the speakers, offering suggestions and, incredibly, criticisms."

John also believed that Paul showed a hidden resentment of Yoko in "Get Back" as evidenced in *The Playboy Interviews.* Lennon stated: "No, I think there's some underlying thing about Yoko in there ['Get Back']. . .you know, 'Get back to where you once belonged.' Every time he sang the line in the studio he'd look at Yoko" (Sheff, 179).

John also favored the double album over George Martin's objections: "I tried to plead with them to be selective and make it a really good single album, but they wouldn't have it" (Dowlding, 220). Possibly, the Beatles considered the release of a double album a reduction in the total number of albums that the group owed EMI. Regardless, Lennon believed that *The White Album* contained his best playing and song writing: "I keep saying that I always preferred the double album, because my music is better on the double album [and] because I'm being myself on it . . .I don't like production so much" (Dowlding, 221).

Probably the Beatle most influenced by the growing riff in the band was Ringo Starr. He became the first Beatle to quit the group during the recording of *The White Album.* It was common knowledge that Paul not only took a stronger hand in this album's production, but that he played a great number of the drum parts as well. Ringo came into the studio one day and simply pretended that he hadn't noticed that his drum tracks had been removed and that McCartney had laid down his own tracks in Ringo's place. It seemed that Ringo couldn't quite get the drum feel to "Back In The USSR" and Paul recorded it himself.

Paul: "I'm sure it pissed Ringo off when he couldn't quite get the drums to 'Back In The USSR.' and I sat in. It's very weird to know that you can do a thing someone else is having trouble with. If you go down and do it, just bluff right through it, you think, 'What the hell -- at least I'm helping.' Then the paranoia comes in: 'But I'm going to show him up!' I was very sensitive to that" (*Musician*, October, 1986).

After Paul criticized Ringo's drumming, Ringo left the group. Ringo stated: "I felt like I was playing like shit. And those three were really getting on. I had this feeling that nobody loved me. I felt horrible. So I said to myself, 'What am I doing here? Those three are getting along so well and I'm not even playing well.' That was madness, so I went away on holiday to sort things out. I don't know, maybe I was just paranoid. You know that to play in a band you have to trust each other" (Dowlding, 218).

While Ringo was gone, the other Beatles begged him to reconsider his decision. According to McCartney, "[After] two days of us telling him he was the greatest drummer in the world for the Beatles -- which I believe -- he came back [supposedly to find his drums covered in flowers]" (Dowlding, 218).

William Dowlding gave this history of the cover's concept: "The album has a white cover. On early copies the name Beatles was embossed on its front; later it was simply printed in light-gray type. The design was suggested by artist Richard Hamilton. He said the Beatles should make the cover design distinctive by having no design at all on it. But he thought the white cover should be defaced in some way and suggested that the albums be consequently numbered as would a limited edition of a piece of art. The Beatles asked Gordon House to design the album package using Hamilton's ideas. . .Pete Shotton said it was McCartney's idea to stamp each copy of the album with an individual number. McCartney originally wanted to hold a lottery with those numbers; he thought it would be a strong marketing gimmick. But he came to the conclusion that it would make the Beatles seem cheap."

The endless search for Paul's death clues, however, would be an extremely effective marketing idea! Beatles fans once again rushed out to the record stores in great numbers to purchase the older albums and look for the hidden answers about the great tragedy.

Some fans believed the color white was symbolic of the traditional color of mourning in many countries. In this case, the remaining Beatles were giving yet another clue: they missed their departed friend.

The White Album was released in Great Britain on November 22, 1968, while it was released in the United States on November 25, 1968. The US advance orders alone numbered 1.9 million copies. By the end of 1970, the album sold over 6.5 million copies which made it the best selling double-album of all time. This, however, changed in 1977 with the release of the Saturday Night Fever soundtrack (Dowlding, 216).

Apparently, The White Album was at least more popular with George and Ringo than Sgt. Pepper's. Lennon suggested that he thought his playing was better on this recording.

As magnifying glasses scrutinized every corner and shadow of the Beatle photo fold-out, investigators again found pertinent clues to fan the flames of the "Paul Is Dead" hysteria. The album contained full face shots of the Beatles individually. Three of the Beatles (John, George, and

----

Ringo) posed similarly. Once again, McCartney's photo was different. Paul's picture was a more detailed close-up than the other three, and under closer inspection, it became apparent that there were scars above McCartney's lip -- scars that had not been present in earlier photographs. Could these scars represent the after effects of the car accident, or the tell-tale signs of plastic surgery? Did this suggest that the Beatles had replaced Paul?

A picture of Paul McCartney with ghost-like skeletal hands that seemed to reach out to grab him appeared in the lower right hand corner of the photo spread containing the song lyrics. Could this mean that Paul had fallen victim to the icy coldness of Death?

Also, there is a photograph of McCartney in a bathtub with his head underwater, which many investigators believed was another hint at McCartney's alleged decapitation. The British Press was similarly shocked when they noticed a picture of McCartney in the nude (behind a cleverly and strategically located column of white). Obviously, the Beatles had prepared yet another montage of photographs which many fans claimed laid another foundation for even more cryptic clues.

As usual, most emphasis centered around the songs and the song lyrics themselves. In the song "Glass Onion" the lyric "Here's another clue for you all. The walrus was Paul" could have meant that the hoaxer was Paul. Remember, it was the walrus who misled the oysters: "'O oysters, come and walk with us!' The walrus did beseech. 'A pleasant walk, a pleasant talk, along the briny beach: We cannot do with more than four, to give an hand to each'" (Carroll, *Through The Looking Glass*). In this case, if the walrus were Paul, it only stood to reason that the carpenter was Lennon. Together they could have deceived the gullible press and the public who heard what they wanted to hear and saw what they wanted to see.

This explanation would give John the chance to symbolically and indirectly represent Christ as the carpenter. During the making of "Revolution 9," John Lennon announced to his friend Pete Shotton that he [Lennon] was actually Jesus Christ. This occurred near dawn and during an LSD trip. Lennon then called the other Beatles, as well as business associates at Apple, and immediately broke the news to them. The stunned neo-disciples were shocked, and perhaps a little irate about being disturbed from their sleep by such a revelation. They announced that they needed more time to consider this oracle (Dowlding, 248).

Lennon appeared to be sincere in this belief. Perhaps, this was significant in his choosing of the Christ symbol. However, the carpenter's task has always been to construct, and perhaps John was carpenter-like in his creation and building of one of the greatest hoaxes on the public. Did we, like the foolish oysters, accept this bizarre premise blindly? Where was the concrete evidence that common sense demanded? Wasn't it time for the cold hard facts? Where was the body?

The reference from Lewis Carroll's conversation between the walrus and the oysters ("we cannot do with more than four") may have intricately related to the four Beatle albums under discussion: *Sgt. Pepper's*, *Magical Mystery Tour*, *The White Album*, and *Abbey Road*. These four albums contained the bulk of the death clues under scrutiny. This would be appropriate in a Carrollian manner in which Lennon directly referred back to the exact number of clue-bearing albums. These albums, like oysters, had to be opened and examined closely to find what pearls of wisdom the Beatles had placed to enlighten their fans.

"Glass Onion" also contained other references to Beatle songs convincing many fans that these songs contained other clues to Paul's death. In the first verse Lennon sings: "I told you about Strawberry Fields. You know the place where nothing is real." To many listeners, the phrase "Strawberry Fields" was reminiscent of the eerie phrase "I buried Paul."

The line "nothing is real" refers to the Beatle movie promo of "Strawberry Fields Forever." In the promo, whenever the line "nothing is real" is mentioned, Paul's face appears, suggesting that this is not the face of the real McCartney.

Lennon also sings "looking through the bent back tulips to see how the other half lives, looking through a glass onion." Did the bent back tulips represent the flowers around the drum skin on the *Sgt. Pepper's* cover? Did "to see how the other half lives" suggest the mysterious look alike -- the other half of Paul McCartney? Perhaps the other half referred to a reflection of reality, the alter-ego of Paul McCartney -- William Campbell. In the second verse, John tells us that the walrus was Paul and "Lady Madonna, trying to meet ends meet, yeah." Remember that in "Lady Madonna" the "Wednesday morning papers didn't come." To some, this may have hinted at a news blackout that hid the tragic consequences from an unknowing world. Even the phrase "Glass Onion" may suggest looking at the *Sgt. Pepper's* drum skin through a looking glass in the same sense that both an onion and a drum have a skin

----

John sings that he is also "fixing a hole in the ocean." I'm sure that many fans remembered the strange Be At Leso clue and were convinced that John was referring once again to Paul's watery grave.

Ringo Starr also contributed a song to *The White Album*. The song, "Don't Pass Me By" actually reached the number one hit position in Scandinavia. Many sleuths heard evidence of the tragic automobile crash in the song's last verse: "I'm sorry that I doubted you. I was so unfair. You were in a car crash and you lost your hair. You said you'd be late, about an hour or two. I said that's alright. I'm waiting here just waiting to hear from you." The car crash in which the victim lost his hair reinforces the decapitation theory. Mentioning the terms "doubting" and "unfair" might have suggested the tension that arose between the Beatles -- specifically between Paul and Ringo. The reference to being late, "about an hour or two," could have suggested the original theory that McCartney left Abbey Road studios angrily on a "stupid bloody Tuesday" and "blew his mind out in a car." All of this had occurred on November 9, 1966.

Perhaps the most haunting song on *The White Album* was "While My Guitar Gently Weeps" by George Harrison. Harrison stated, "This idea was in my head when I visited my parents' house in the North of England. I decided to write a song based on the first thing I saw upon opening any book -- as it would be relative to that moment, at that time. I picked a book at random, opened it -- saw 'gently weeps' -- then laid the book down again and started the song" (*I Me Mine*).

According to Harrison, the reactions of the other Beatles were less than enthusiastic: "I worked on that song with John, Paul, and Ringo one day, and they were not interested in it at all. And I knew inside of me that it was a nice song. The next day I was with Eric [Clapton], and I was going into the session, and I said, 'We're going to do this song. Come on and play on it.' He said, 'Oh, no. I can't do that. Nobody ever plays on the Beatles' records.' I said, 'Look, it's my song, and I want you to play on it.' So Eric came in, and the other guys were as good as gold -- because he was there. Also, it left me free to just play the rhythm and do the vocal. So Eric played that, and I thought it was really good. Then we listened to it back, and he said, 'Ah, there's a problem, though; it's not Beatley enough' -- so we put it through the ADT [automatic double tracker] to wobble it a bit" (*Guitar*, November, 1987).

The strange imagery of a bluesy guitar that wept in somber melodic strains was compelling. The lines "I look at the world and I notice

----

its turning" could have simply meant that life continued. In this case, the Beatles struggled onward as a group following the tragic death of one of its members. At the conclusion of the song, many sleuths heard Harrison's softly-moaning voice exclaim "Paul, Paul" sadly during the song's fade-out. This longing voice could well have convinced some listeners that this was yet another clue to McCartney's death, as a distraught George Harrison remembered his fallen partner.

The Beatles were pioneers when it came to avant-garde experiments with previously untried recording techniques. The Beatles, for instance, were the first group to record backward passages in their music. John, in particular, was adamant about the use of backward tracks. The public today is only too aware of supposed backward masking techniques. The religious right has held countless seminars to acquaint today's youth with hidden Satanic messages. Led Zeppelin's "Stairway to Heaven" has always been popular airway fare on dark and gloomy Halloween nights as radio disc jockeys across the country astonish their listeners by playing the hidden message "My sweet Satan." It is debatable whether there are secret, dark, and mysterious messages on certain albums. Some rock groups actually increased their record sales when they denied the hidden messages contained in their recordings.

There are a number of critics who also claimed that the Beatles were also influenced by Satanism. After all, Aleister Crowley, The Great Beast, was included on the *Sgt. Pepper's* album cover. Allegedly, the Mark of the Beast [666] written in red appeared upon Crowley's forehead upon close examination. The use of Satanic symbolism perhaps reminded critics of the archetype of the Devil's sacrifice -- the death of a member of a coven in exchange for wealth and success. This theory may have suggested that the Beatles offered McCartney as a sacrificial rite for fame and fortune as the Rolling Stones offered Brian Jones. As a further coincidence, one Rolling Stones album was entitled *Her Satanic Majesty's Request*. What could have been this macabre request?

Many believers were sure that Satan's request was the blood of Brian Jones. Tragedy has always seemed to stalk rock and roll bands. For instance, the untimely, tragic deaths of Bon Scot of AC/DC, Duane Allman of the Allman Brothers Band, Randy Rhodes from Ozzy Osborne's band, Keith Moon of The Who, Jimi Hendrix, Janis Joplin, Jim Morrison, and Kurt Cobain, as well as countless others, fit this archetypal

----

description. It seems that rock and roll has its own recurring ghost stories, so much the better for modern urban legends.

The first backward vocal track performed by the Beatles was in the song "Rain." Lennon remembered the concept behind "Rain": "That's me again -- with the first backwards tape on any record anywhere. Before Hendrix, before The Who. . .I got home from the studio and I was stoned out of my mind on marijuana and, as I usually do, I listened to what I'd recorded that day. Somehow I got it on backwards and I sat there, transfixed, with the earphones on, with a big hash joint. I ran in the next day and said, 'I know what to do with it, I know. . .listen to this!' So I made them all play it backwards. The fade is me actually singing backwards with the guitars going backwards. 'Sharethsmnowthsmeaness'" (Sheff, 175-6).

Actually, Lennon sang: "Rain. When the rain comes they run and hide their heads." George Martin also remembered, "Once you started something, for a while it almost became the fashion. For example, once I'd turned John's voice around on 'Rain,' played his voice backward to him and put it on the track, it was 'Great! Let's try everything backward!' So George started doing backward guitar solos, there was a backward cymbal on 'Strawberry Fields,' until that was exhausted and it was on to the next gimmick. It was a healthy curiosity to find new sounds and new ways of expressing themselves" (*Musician*, July, 1987/ Dowlding, 129).

Once the thrill of backward tracking became commonplace, the Beatles utilized this technique as a vehicle for disguising death clues in their songs. The first instance is found just after "I'm So Tired" and just before "Blackbird." It seemed appropriate that this message appeared in this particular location since a blackbird [raven] in literature has always served as a symbol of approaching death. For example, in Shakespeare's *Macbeth,* Lady Macbeth referred to a raven that signaled the approach of King Duncan. Edgar Allen Poe's "The Raven" forced the poet to contemplate the eternity of death "that will be lifted nevermore."

Coincidentally, perhaps, there are several Poe references in Beatles history. First of all, a gloomy Edgar Allen Poe stood among the crowd on the *Sgt. Pepper's* album jacket. In "I Am The Walrus," John Lennon sang, "Man you should have seen them kicking Edgar Allen Poe."

Poe wrote a series of columns dealing with the solution of secret ciphers for a Philadelphia newspaper, *The Alexander's Weekly Messenger.* As Poe's fame grew, so did his reading public. Possibly his

----

greatest cryptic work was called "The Goldbug" and contained secret messages that had to be decoded by his readers. Poe's motifs centered around the themes of burial alive and the return from the dead. This concept played nicely with the Beatle mystery since Poe's portrait appeared at a staged funeral which may have been premature. Was Paul like Ligeia and destined to return from the dead in another body -- that of an impostor? Or could the Beatle conspiracy have referred to the first great detective novel, Poe's *Purloined Letter*? In this work, the condemning clues were in front of the police at all times; nothing was hidden. The answer to the mystery could only be solved through careful deduction and close observation. Wouldn't it be just as proper for the Beatles to purloin their albums with mysterious clues and place them directly under the noses, and ears, of the public where they have been virtually unnoticed for over twenty years? What inspiration! Poe, as well as Lewis Carroll, who also delighted in designing puzzles and mysteries, would have indeed approved of such clever deception. The Beatles, through modern day recordings, were able to produce many more cryptic sensory clues than Poe and Carroll's jumbled visual symbols.

The hidden backward message followed "I'm So Tired" with John Lennon singing: "I'd give you everything I've got for a little peace of mind." The strange murmuring sounds are faint and obviously recorded backwards. According to Mark Lewisohn's *The Beatles: Recording Sessions*, Lennon, when questioned about these strange mutterings, actually whispered, "Monsieur, monsieur, how about another one?" After countless listenings it remained doubtful that this was the actual message. However, when the track was reversed, it sounded like: "Paul Is Dead now, miss him, miss him, miss him." This mysterious voice softly uttered Paul's melancholy obituary. Other listeners claim that the voice says, "Paul is a dead man, miss him, miss him, miss him."

Though this reversed message was indeed bizarre, it was nothing compared to the chilling revelations of "Revolution 9," which ironically would be voted the most unpopular Beatles' track in a poll by *Village Voice* (Dowlding, 249). George Harrison confided that he hardly ever listened to it. George Martin, along with Paul and Ringo, tried to keep the song off *The White Album*. But Lennon had a different opinion. Lennon stated after the recording: "This is the music of the future. You can forget all the rest of the shit we've done -- this is it! Everybody will be making this stuff one day -- you don't even have to know how to play a musical instrument to do it!" (Dowlding, 249).

John Lennon described the making of "Revolution 9": "Well, the slow version of 'Revolution' on the album went on and on and on and I took the fade-out part, which is what they sometimes do with disco records now, and just layered all this stuff over it. It has the basic rhythm of the original 'Revolution' going on with some twenty loops we put on, things from the archives of EMI. We were cutting up classical music and making different-size loops, and then I got an engineer tape on which some test engineer was saying, 'Number nine, number nine, number nine.' All those different bits of sound and noises are all compiled. There were some ten machines with people holding pencils on the loops -- some only inches long and some a yard long. I fed them all in and mixed them live. I did a few mixes until I got one I liked. Yoko was there for the whole thing and she made decisions about the loops to use. It was somewhat under her influence, I suppose. Once I heard her stuff -- not just the screeching and the howling but her sort of word pieces and talking and breathing and all this strange stuff, I thought, My God, I got intrigued, so I wanted to do one. I spent more time on 'Revolution Nine' than I did on half the other songs I ever wrote. It was a montage" (Sheff, 167).

John was right. It was a montage of sounds. As the recording started, the test engineer dutifully and monotonously repeated, "Number nine, number nine" over and over again thirteen times until the voice faded out into a void of sounds. Symbolically, the clue had to do with the number nine. Could the nine possibly be related to the mysterious date of the accident -- November the ninth? Perhaps the clue had to do instead with the singling out of the victim. By counting the letters of the Beatles' last names, sleuths discovered that S-t-a-r-r contained five letters (S-t-a-r-k-e-y had seven letters), L-e-n-n-o-n was made up of six letters, H-a-r-r-i-s-o-n possessed eight characters, but only M-c-C-a-r-t-n-e-y fit the correct pattern with exactly nine letters. Was this yet another attempt to identify the corpse?

In *Lennon*, Ray Coleman mentioned a series of symbolic nines that controlled Lennon's fate: "John was acutely aware of the fact that the number nine had dominated his life. He was born on October 9, 1940. Sean was born on October 9, 1975. Brian Epstein first saw John and the Beatles at Liverpool's Cavern on November 9, 1961, and he secured their record contract with EMI in London on May 9, 1962. The debut record,

'Love Me Do,' was on Parlophone R4949. John met Yoko Ono on November 9, 1966. John and Yoko's apartment was located on West 72nd Street, New York City (seven plus two making nine), and their main Dakota apartment number was also, at first 72. The bus he traveled on as a student each morning from his home to Liverpool Art College had been the 72. John's songs included 'Revolution 9,' '#9 Dream,' and 'One After 909,' which he had written at his mother's home at 9 Newcastle [nine letters] Road, Wavertree [nine letters], Liverpool [nine letters]." Also add that his prolific songwriting partner's last name was McCartney [nine letters], that Brian Epstein died on August 27, 1967 [two and seven again making nine], and John himself was pronounced dead at 9th Avenue New York City just minutes before the start of a new day, December the 9th. Of course Lennon's murder occurred on the night of December the eighth, but since he was an Englishman, the time in England would have been five hours earlier and his death actually occurred on December the ninth in Great Britain.

Coleman's observations suggested new meanings to the great hoax. It would be grand if the Beatles followed in the steps of William Shakespeare, another English master lyricist, and died on their birthday. If Epstein discovered the group on November 9, 1961, and rocketed them to fame and fortune, then the release of *Sgt. Pepper's* could very well have signaled not only the symbolic death of the group but a rebirth of four unique individuals who now had very little in common, but nonetheless worked diligently until they developed their own different musical styles. In this state, the Beatles would have come full circle and achieved what Carl Jung referred to as "the ultimate state of oneness." This symbolic circle could be related to the Yin-Yang principle -- the ever present mixture of light and darkness, and masculine and feminine traits that denoted the cosmic energies of the universe (Cirlot, 47-8).

According to G.A. Gaskell's *Dictionary Of All Scriptures And Myths*, the number nine in Far Eastern Indian symbolism "relates to the number three, the number of perfection and completeness. Nine, which is of course three squared, refers to the attainment of perfection on the three lower planes."

In *A Dictionary Of Symbols*, Cirlot notes that the number nine is "the end-limit of the numerical series before its return to unity. For the Hebrews it was a symbol of truth, being characterized by the fact that, when multiplied, it reproduces itself. . .In medicinal rites, it is the

----

symbolic number par excellence, for it represents triple synthesis, that is, the deposition on each plane of the corporal, the intellectual, and the spiritual."

This Far Eastern concept of death and rebirth also related to "Niflheim, the shadowy region of death -- the ninth world. The object of existence is the formation and growth of the soul which is immortal while its lower vehicles are subject to decay and extinction while the soul is being purified stage by stage. The purified souls or individualities shall rise from the lower planes by the unpurified personalities and shall continue to re-incarnate below until they are perfected" (Gaskell, 535).

This could possibly apply to the reincarnation of the Beatles as a new group with a new identity, as well as the new musical direction, which was certainly evident with *Sgt. Pepper's*.

The duality of November 9, 1966, was another strange coincidence. Paul's tragic accident occurred on the same date that John Lennon met Yoko Ono. This was ironic since Yoko Ono is often blamed for the Beatle break-up. In this case, the drum epitaph was actually precognition -- the exact prediction of the beginning of the Beatle death throes!

The strange case of "Revolution 9," which credited Paul McCartney as co-writer, began with the test engineer's droning voice repeating "Number nine, number nine, number nine." As the narration continued, other discordant sounds -- radio broadcasts, sirens, applause, gunfights, sports cheers, the sound of crackling fire, screams, a baby gurgling, a choir singing, and other unidentifiable sounds -- are introduced into the malaise.

William Poundstone's *Big Secrets* contained the following observations: "For this investigation, 'Revolution 9' was transcribed four times, twice on each stereo channel. One copy of each of the tracks was reversed. The four resulting versions were compared against each other and against the original two-channel version. 'Revolution 9' contains a lot of talking. Played in stereo, forward, the longest stretch of understandable speech is probably an announcer saying '. . .every one of them knew that as time went by they'd get a little bit older and a little bit slower. . .(this occurs at approximately 1:05 into the track). . .one believable instance of reversed speech occurs -- someone saying 'Let me out! Let me out!' (once thought to represent McCartney in his totaled Aston Martin). Two iffy reversals occur on the backward recording of the right stereo track: 'She

----

used to be assistant' and 'There were two men. . .' Neither is clear enough or long enough to be convincing. Some of the music, including the recurring theme, sounds more natural in reverse. 'Turn me on, dead man' [the test engineer's lines of 'number nine, number nine' played backward] is a typical phonetic reversal. The forward 'number nine' (repeated throughout the cut) is clear; the reversal is slurred -- something like 'turn me on dedmun.' It has been claimed that 'number nine' must be pronounced with a British accent or with some careful inflection in order to reverse to 'Turn me on dead man.' This seems not to be so. As an experiment, three American-accent renderings of 'number nine' were reversed. All sounded about as much like 'Turn me on, dead man' as the record did. Like the other phonetic reversals, 'Turn me on, dead man' must be considered a coincidence. Much of 'Revolution 9' is on one stereo track only. Near the end a voice says, 'A fine natural imbalance. . .the Watusi, the twist. . .Eldorado. . .Eldorado.' 'A fine natural imbalance' is on the right track only, though the words that follow are in stereo. One of the longer bits of speech -- 'Who could tell what he was saying? His voice was low and his [unintelligible] was high and his eyes were low' -- is clear on the left track, a bare whisper on the right. There is a stereophonically concealed 'secret message' on 'Revolution 9.' The words are on the right track. They begin about four minutes, fifty-eight seconds into the cut and run for about twenty-two seconds. They are not likely to be noticed in stereo because of the much louder left track. The sound of applause begins on the left track at about five minutes, one second into the cut. Deafening noises -- the clapping, sirens, music -- continue on the left track until five minutes, forty seconds. It may or may not have been Lennon's and Ono's intention to conceal the spoken passage. Given the haphazard quality of 'Revolution 9,' the concealment may have been accidental. To recover the passage, the left track must be switched off. The right track can then be heard to contain a sound like a stopwatch ticking, behind these words: 'So the wife called, and we better go see a surgeon. . .[a scream muffles a line that sounds like 'Well, what with the prices, the prices have snowballed, no wonder it's closed]. . .so any and all, he went to see the dentist instead, who gave him a pair of teeth, which wasn't any good at all. So instead of that he joined the bloody navy and went to sea'" (Poundstone, 210-2).

Life magazine's "Magical McCartney Mystery" contained a further transcription: "If the whole band of 'Revolution 9' is reversed, the

---

horrifying sounds of a traffic accident, a bad one, too, emerge: a collision, crackling flames, a voice crying, 'Get me out, get me out!' If the piece is taped stereophonically and then reversed, this is what is heard on one of the four tracks: 'He hit a pole! We better get him to see a surgeon. [Scream.] So anyhow, he went to see a dentist instead. They gave him a pair of teeth that weren't any good at all so -- [A car horn blares.] -- my wings are broken and so is my hair [maybe a reference to Ringo's 'Don't Pass Me By': 'You were in a car crash and you lost your hair.'] I'm not in the mood for words. [Gurgling, battle sounds.] Find the night watchman. A fine natural imbalance. Must have got it in the shoulder blades.'"

As the reader must surely now be aware, not everyone heard the same message, but there are some phrases that seemed to be agreed upon. This may have provided further evidence that we heard what we wanted to hear and that our imaginations had to fill in the pieces of the mysterious puzzle. Many researchers interpreted Poundstone's "So the wife called and we better go see a surgeon" as "So alright Paul, then we had better go and see a surgeon." This occurs approximately five minutes into the track.

The backward track of "Get Me Out" occurs between tape counter positions 058-062. Perhaps the strangest occurrence is where a voice states at 6:43 seconds into the track "Take this brother, may it serve you well." Was this another attempt at providing more fuel to the already blazing funeral pyre of Paul McCartney?

The reference to "Turn me on, dead man" may have been a reference to Lennon's earlier statement concerning the writing of "A Day In The Life." According to Lennon, "Paul's contribution was the beautiful little lick in the song, 'I'd love to turn you on,' that he'd had floating around in his head and couldn't use" (Sheff, 164). Could this be another hint that this line was another attempt at identifying the dead man as Paul McCartney?

CHAPTER 7

Charles Manson's Helter Skelter, The Beatles, And The Strange Case Of William Campbell

Not surprisingly, more than death clue advocates were influenced by *The White Album*. Charles Manson, who had established himself as Jesus Christ incarnate to his believing family, also developed a theory concerning the symbolic meaning of *The White Album*. Manson believed that the Beatles were actually angels sent by God to reveal the secrets of the terrible approaching apocalypse. This apocalypse foretold in the Biblical book of *Revelation* (the *New Testament* book of prophecy) was interpreted by the Manson family to suggest the Beatle song "Revolution 9." Since "Revolution 9" contained such horrible and bizarre sounds, the family was convinced that the recording was actually the sounds of Armageddon itself.

In the Manson family belief, "Revolution 9" referred to *Revelation*, Chapter 9. In this Biblical book, four angels would be loosed from the Euphrates river to summon the destruction of man: "And the four angels were loosed, which were prepared for an hour, and a day, and a month, and a year, for to slay the third part of men."

Manson believed that this Armageddon would involve a racial war between whites and blacks, and that the Beatles were the four angels prophesied to start the last days of man in the years of the great Tribulation. This racial war was proclaimed "Helter Skelter." Lennon stated: "All that Manson stuff was built 'round George's song about pigs ['Piggies'] and this one, Paul's song ("Helter Skelter") about an English fairground [a playground slide]. It has nothing to do with anything, and least of all to do with me" (Sheff, 178).

According to Manson, the blacks led by the Black Panthers would arise and slaughter the white "Piggies." George Harrison offered this explanation to his song: "'Piggies' is a social comment. I was stuck for one line in the middle until my mother came up with the lyric 'What they need is a damn good whacking!' which is a nice simple way of saying they need a good hiding. It needed to rhyme with 'backing,' 'lacking,' and had absolutely nothing to do with American policemen or California shagnasties!" (Dowlding, 233).

In Vincent Bugliosi and Curt Gentry's *Helter Skelter*, there were still other references cleverly hidden throughout *The White Album*, according to Charles Manson. There was the mention in "Honey Pie" that "my position is tragic, come and show me the magic of your Hollywood song." Manson believed that the Beatles wanted and needed his influence and involvement to help fulfill the deadly prophecy of "Helter Skelter." He was to provide the direction through his magical "Hollywood Song." Later, in the same song, the Beatles continue with "Oh, Honey Pie, you are driving me frantic, sail across the Atlantic to where you belong." The lyric also mentions "I'm in love but I'm lazy" which Manson interpreted that he must make the first contact and lead the world to the brink of the apocalypse. In Vincent Bugliosi's *Helter Skelter*, the author mentions that on many occasions, Manson and his family members placed phone calls to the Beatles' management trying to make contract with the four "angels of revelation." Each of these phone calls was unsuccessful. In "Don't Pass Me By," "Blue Jay Way," and "Yer Blues," the Beatles constantly mention waiting for someone to arrive. Charles Manson thought this to be himself, the incarnation of Jesus Christ and the ultimate invitation for Charlie to become the fifth Beatle as well as the fifth angel to complete the ninth chapter of "Revelation": "And the fifth angel sounded and I saw a star fall from Heaven unto the earth; and to him was given the key of the bottomless pit. . .and they had a king over them, which is the angel of the bottomless pit, whose name in the Hebrew tongue is Abaddon but in the Greek tongue hath his name Apollyon." It was extremely clear to each of Manson's followers that Abaddon and Apollyon were effective aliases for Charlie.

The Manson family had planned to survive the apocalyptic holocaust by hiding out in the desert until the racial war was completed. In the lyrics of "Helter Skelter" the Beatles sing "When I get to the bottom I go back to the top of the slide where I stop and I turn and I go for a ride." Manson interpreted this as his followers emerging from the bottomless pit. The family would arm themselves with machine guns and would convert stolen jeeps into dune buggies. The Manson family would then rise up and forcibly seize power from the blacks. Charles Manson would then rule supreme in his new utopia on earth. For instance, the lyrics to "Revolution 1" mentions "We all want to change the world. . .but when you talk about destruction, don't you know that you can count me out." (Here, a voice saying "in" immediately after the last word "out" can be heard.) The Beatles also mentioned that they would "like to see the plan," which Manson again interpreted as an invitation to provide the Beatles with his plan for "Helter Skelter."

Charles Manson was convinced that his plan would be in the form of an album that he would record with the complete approval of the Beatles to help show the world the "magic of his Hollywood song." Manson interpreted the lyrics to "I Will" as evidence to back his plan: "And when at last I find you, your song will fill the air, sing it loud so I can hear you, make it easy to be near you." He also noticed that at the conclusion of "Piggies" there are a number of oinking sounds followed by the sounds of machine gun fire. This had to be the start of the racial apocalypse.

Manson was a charismatic figure. He, like Stephen Stills of Crosby, Stills, and Nash, was said to have auditioned for a role in a new television production that parodied the Beatles. This new television program was to be called "The Monkees." Stills was rejected because of his bad teeth. Manson possibly was refused for his strange, seemingly psychopathic behavior. Perhaps his grubby appearance did not maximize his chances either.

In *Heroes And Villains,* Steven Gaines tells how Manson, once befriended by Dennis Wilson of The Beach Boys, used this connection to take advantage of Wilson's property and connections. It even seemed that The Beach Boys recorded one of Manson's songs, "Cease to Exist" without Manson's knowledge. This almost prophetic title was changed by the Beach Boys to "Never Learn Not To Love." This song, included on the *20/20* album, was the B-side to the album's first release, "Bluebirds Over The Mountain."

Manson was furious that his lyrics had been changed and that his song had been stolen. His anger also included record producer Terry Melcher, Doris Day's son, whom Manson believed had wrongly denied him a recording contract. It was this catalyst that prompted the family to choose the residents of 10050 Cielo Drive as victims. It didn't matter that Melcher no longer lived in this house. The new resident was Sharon Tate, the pregnant wife of film director Roman Polanski. Her house guests included Jay Sebring, her former boyfriend and popular hairstylist; Abigail Folger, heiress to the Folger coffee fortune; and Voytek Frykowski, Folger's boyfriend. Their innocent deaths provided a chilling warning to Terry Melcher and was a barbaric massacre that sickened the world.

When the police entered the Tate home, the grisly mutilated bodies bore evidence to the savagery of the murderers. The police noticed that the walls were covered in slogans written in the victims' own blood. These slogans read "Helter Skelter," "Political Piggy," and "Arise."

"Helter Skelter" referred to Manson's concept of the approaching racial war leading to Armageddon. The phrase "Political Piggy" bore reference to the victims of such a race war. The last phrase, "Arise" also referred to the upcoming racial war. It seemed that in "Blackbird" (a song Manson believed symbolically stood for the black race, especially the Black Panthers) McCartney sang: "You were only waiting for this moment to arise." This lyric is repeated over and over throughout the song. Manson believed that the blacks had to be shown the method in which to begin the great Apocalypse. They would have to "take these broken wings and learn to fly."

The family committed the murders and led the way to revolution as they demonstrated the proper method for slaughtering the white "piggies." One of the murderers, Susan Atkins, was given the nickname "Sexy Sadie." Perhaps the Manson case served as the ultimate warning for those fans who suffered from acute Beatle mania. It was not always harmless to interpret lyrical meanings. In this case, someone's interpretation proved deadly and was no simple game that provided chills to those listening to the hidden messages in darkness. The Boogie Man had come out of the darkness.

After *The White Album* was released, Paul McCartney envisioned a live Beatle concert. It was time to take the Beatles back on the road and play before their devoted fans. Apple's Derek Taylor went as far as to promise that there would be a concert. However, the friction between the group continued and Paul reminded the other members that they had been "very negative since Mr. Epstein passed away. . .the only way for it not to be a bit of a drag is for the three of us to think, should we make it positive or should we forget it? Mr. Epstein, he said sort of 'get suits on,' and we did. And so we were always fighting that discipline a bit.

But now it's silly to fight that discipline if it's our own. It's self-imposed these days, so we do as little as possible. But I think we need a bit more if we are going to get away with it."

"Well, if that's what doing it is," Harrison snapped back, "I don't want to do anything. . .I don't want to do any of the songs on the show because they always turn out awful like that. They come out like a compromise whereas in the studio they can work on it until you get it how you want it."

Paul and musical director Michael Lindsay-Hogg suggested staging this new concert either at an ancient coliseum in Tunisia ("You know it's just impractical to try and get all these people and equipment there,'" said Harrison); or on a ship in the ocean (Harrison: "Very expensive and insane. . .I don't think you're going to get a perfect acoustic place by the water out of doors.") Lennon offered his own suggestion: "I'm warming to the idea of an asylum" (Schaffner, 117).

When news of this dissension reached the press, the concert was canceled and fifty lucky winners who were supposed to receive tickets to the Beatle concerts received free Beatles albums instead.

The Beatles placed a great deal of pressure on themselves. What direction remained unexplored that could compete with the revolutionary musical synthesis that would produce a rival to *Sgt. Pepper's*? The public expected more. *The Beatle Monthly*, a publication dedicated to news of the Beatles, ran a column by S.C. Blake, who wrote: "Do the fans want to go backward into the Rock 'n' Roll era? Do we want the simple run-of-the-mill sound of three guitars and a drum kit? Surely the Beatles shouldn't stop experimenting with new sounds! Why don't they look to the future instead of 1962?" (Schaffner, 117).

The Beatles had indeed looked to the future. Other changes helped distance the group from themselves as well as from their adoring public. John Lennon and his wife Cynthia were divorced and Lennon married Yoko Ono. John believed that marriage was not necessary but that a "Happening" could result from their marriage. John's experimentation with the avant-garde continued with his recordings made with Yoko. Long tracks of her screaming vocals accompanied only by John's electric guitar feeding-back in equally frenzied tones led *Rolling Stone* to suggest that the new sounds were "like a severely retarded child being tortured."

John experimented with his own backing group which he called The Plastic Ono Band and recorded the politically relevant "Give Peace A

Chance." The Lennons staged 'bed-ins,' 'hair peace,' took out billboard ads that stated "War is over if you want it -- John and Yoko," and suggested that each world leader be given acorns to plant and grow the seeds of world peace.

John and Yoko recorded "The Ballad of John And Yoko" which commemorated their social revolution. This song was rushed into production with only John and Paul performing on the track. The song did not receive extensive radio play in the United States, however, since the chorus included the refrain, "Christ, you know it ain't easy." This phrase reminded American disc jockeys of Lennon's earlier remarks about Christ. Of course with Brian Epstein now dead, John repeated his original comment concerning Christ. He stated that he was "Christ's biggest fan" and that "Yes, I still think it. Kids are more influenced by us than by Jesus" (Schaffner, 122).

This strange behavior only alienated John further from the group and created a puzzle for his old, unchanging fans. George Harrison immersed himself in Far Eastern musical forms and recorded songs dealing with his involvement with Hare Krishna. He also released a solo album entitled *Electronic Sound.* According to one music critic, the solo offerings of Lennon and Harrison were "unfit for human ears."

Ringo became more interested in the acting profession and landed a movie role in Terry Southern's *Candy.* He also was involved with Peter Sellers in *The Magic Christian.* Of course, John Lennon had maintained that Ringo was the best actor of all. These dramatic changes now pulled the Beatles in their separate directions, but the unthinkable was yet to happen. Stranger than the death clues that shook the media was the startling revelation that on March 12, 1969, Paul McCartney married Linda Eastman. Young women throughout the world mourned his passing from bachelorhood. Now all the Beatles were married.

Paul's marriage was not wholly unexpected, but everyone was sure that the lucky girl would be his long time love and fiancée, Jane Asher. As the death clues surfaced, many fans pointed to this marriage as proof that this McCartney was truly an impostor. The rumors suggested that the McCartney look-alike, William Campbell, or Billy Shears, married the girl of his own choice and the remaining members of the Beatles paid a huge cash settlement to a heartbroken Jane Asher, ensuring her silence concerning the death of the real McCartney.

Linda Eastman was a successful photographer whose pictures of the Beatles and other rock bands appeared throughout the rock music fan magazines. McCartney, the family man, secluded himself from the crowds and recorded his first solo album, *McCartney*.

Although these solo projects were being carried out by the Beatles as individuals, the group was busy recording songs for the *Let It Be* album. This LP was postponed and later produced by Phil Spector, but was not released until one year after the Beatle break-up. *Let It Be* proved uncharacteristic of the famous Beatle sounds. For the first time in the group's history, female backing voices were to be used on Beatle tracks. Paul McCartney was furious with the over-production of "The Long And Winding Road" which he had considered another "Yesterday." This only served to increase the tremendous strain between the members.

The Beatles brought along a movie crew to film the recording of the *Let It Be* soundtrack. The mounting tension was evident to the onlooker. In interviews from *The Beatles Complete*, George Martin remembered the turbulent recordings: "In order to get things together, Paul would try to get everybody organized and would be rather over-bossy, which the other boys would dislike. But it was the only way of getting together. John would go wafting away with Yoko. George would say he wouldn't be coming in the following day. It was just a general disintegration -- disenchantment if you like."

George Harrison recalled: "This cooperation [his involvement with other musicians in America] contrasted dramatically with the superior attitude which for years Paul had shown toward me musically. In normal circumstances, I had not let this attitude bother me and, to get a peaceful life, I had always let him have his own way, even when this meant that songs which I had composed were not being recorded. When I came back from the United States I was in a very happy frame of mind, but I quickly discovered that I was up against the same old Paul. . .in front of the cameras, as we were actually being filmed, Paul started to get at me about the way I was playing" (Dowlding, 254).

Harrison, in a *Crawdaddy* interview dated February, 1977, added: "There's a scene where Paul and I are having an argument. . .and we're trying to cover it up. Then the next scene I'm not there, and Yoko's just screaming, doing her screeching number. Well, that's where I'd left and I went home and wrote "Wah-Wah." It'd given me a wah-wah [headache], like I had such a headache with that whole argument, it was just a headache." Dowlding notes that George's "Wah-Wah--Wah-Wah -- you've given me a wah-wah" later appeared on Harrison's *All Things Must Pass.*

Most of us could not imagine what pulled the Beatles so far apart, but the answer was not terribly hard to comprehend. The answer was mainly financial. The Beatles' Apple Corps Productions lost great sums of money. Lennon complained that the Beatles faced certain bankruptcy. Since Epstein's death, the Beatles fortunes dwindled. There were too many people on the Beatle payroll, but the group could not come to an agreement on who their new business manager should be.

At this stage, Allen Klein came into the Beatles' lives. Klein, a successful businessman, especially appealed to John Lennon. Perhaps this was due to Klein's early life which resembled that of Lennon. Lennon commented: "He [Klein] not only knew my work, and the lyrics I had written, but he also understood them. . .he told me what was happening with the Beatles, and my relationship with Paul and George and Ringo. He knew every damn thing about us" (Schaffner, 123).

John, Ringo, and George were determined that Klein should handle their business affairs, while Paul insisted that his new father-in-law, Lee Eastman, be the new business manager. The Beatle wars continued. The financial rewards for this position were overwhelming. Brian Epstein's estate received twenty-five percent of all total Beatles funds. The right man could easily make millions of dollars.

Klein ruled Apple. He cut everything that was not indispensable. Paul McCartney and John Lennon were influenced to write "You Never Give Me Your Money" in honor of the financial crisis. Allen Klein, however, managed at least one financial plum -- he negotiated EMI records into an increased royalty rate of sixty-nine cents per album. This rate was unheard of at the time and raised the retail cost of an American LP to seven dollars (Schaffner, 123).

This may have helped win Paul over to Klein's side as the financial situation improved somewhat, but the tension between band members remained. One day John Lennon visited Paul McCartney and informed him that it was over and that he wanted a divorce. John no longer wanted to be a Beatle.

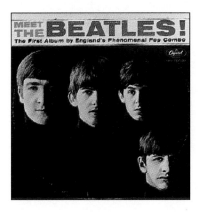
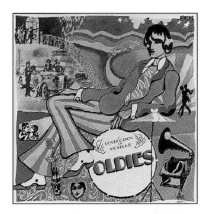

This Great Britain import was released shortly before *Sgt. Pepper's,* and, to many fans, contained yet another bass drum clue to Paul's tragic accident. The shadowy figure's head brings back memories of Robert Freeman's *Meet The Beatles (With The Beatles).* Notice the figure's shadowy face is in the same location as Paul's and, if you look closely, you can see a car that appears to be running off the road into the figure's head.

Some investigators claimed that Paul's profile appeared to be haphazardly pieced in with the other Beatles' full-face portraits.

Some overzealous fans noticed that Paul was portrayed differently from the other members of the group as far back as the *Help* LP; he is the only one not wearing a hat.

Some death-clue advocates claimed that this title may have represented the fatal car accident, and that the Beatles, with somber faces, were looking down into a grave or coffin.

This infamous banned cover demonstrated the Beatles' macabre sense of humor. Not only was it a statement about their concerns about the American packaging of their albums, it also hinted at some death clues. Note the headless dolls, the false teeth. Remember – it was the Beatles' first actual cover-up!

In this photo, three of the Beatles gather around Paul sitting in an open trunk. Some fans suggested that the death clues originated here. Turned on its side, the open trunk looks like a coffin.

This album cover provided a majority of clues that led fans to suggest that McCartney had been killed in an automobile accident, and subsequently replaced by an impostor. Notice the open hand over Paul's head and the waxen images of the Beatles looking down on the grave.

The yellow hyacinth plants appear to spell out "Paul?"

This doll appears to have a small Aston-Martin convertible resting upon her right leg. The doll sits in the lap of a stuffed grandmother figure wearing a blood-stained driving glove on her left hand.

The innocent-looking drumskin that we have known and loved for over twenty-seven years contains the most bizarre clue in the "Paul Is Dead" hysteria.

By holding a straight-edged mirror perpendicular to the center of "Lonely Hearts," a hidden message appears.

The drumskin, designed by Joe Ephgrave states, through the mirror's reflection, "I One IX He <> Die." This is a direct reference to the fatal car crash of November 9, 1966 (11-9-66) and the arrow points directly at the victim (McCartney) and to the flower-covered grave where he supposedly now lies.

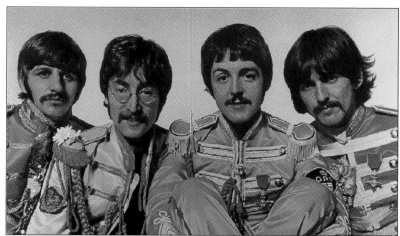

Paul McCartney wears a black arm band which appears to read "OPD." Many fans interpreted OPD to suggest British police jargon for "Officially Pronounced Dead."

George Harrison points to the opening line from "She's Leaving Home." The lyric states: "Wednesday morning at five o'clock as the day begins." This is another reference to Paul McCartney's accident on November 9, 1966, an accident which reportedly occurred on a Wednesday morning at 5 AM!

Here we have one of the Beatles in the black walrus costume. Notice the gold-rimmed glasses on the figure at the top right. Some researchers believe that by looking at the album cover upside down in a mirror, one can discern a phone number that, when dialed, will explain the truth behind the rumors. (Good luck!)

Blue Jay Way
George Harrison 3:50

Your Mother Should Know
John Lennon-Paul McCartney 2:33

I Am the Walrus
(" *No you're not!* " said **Little Nicola**)
John Lennon-Paul McCartney 4:35
All side-one selections are
published by Comet Music Corp., ASCAP

...plus these other selections

Little Nicola lets John know that he isn't the walrus.

Again, Paul is shown with an open hand over his head – a scene that is duplicated on the *Yellow Submarine* cover.

In the film *Magical Mystery Tour,* Paul, dressed in a military uniform, sits behind a sign that reads "I WAS." The flags are reportedly crossed in the manner of a military funeral.

This fishbowl photo does not appear in the film. The rumor is that if you hold the picture at an angle, the lady's beret becomes one of the eye sockets of a skull.

Three of the Beatles wear red carnations, yet Paul's is black! If you look closely, you can see that the flowers look as if they were painted on the Beatles' lapels. So much for luckily finding one back-stage!

In this shot from the booklet contained within *Magical Mystery Tour,* we see Paul bare-foot in his socks. If you look to the right of Ringo's drumhead (which reads "Love the 3 Beatles") you can see an empty pair of shoes which appear to be covered in blood. In this case as well as in one other photo within the booklet, Paul appeared barefoot well over a year before the *Abbey Road* cover.

In this scene, John stands next to a sign which reads, "The best way to go is by M&D Company." The rumor suggested that the M&D Company was a funeral home in Great Britain.

The White Album seemed to be a reference to the traditional color of mourning in some societies.

This photograph of Paul in disguise led many fans to believe that the Beatles had actually included a photo of the impostor Billy Shears, or William Campbell.

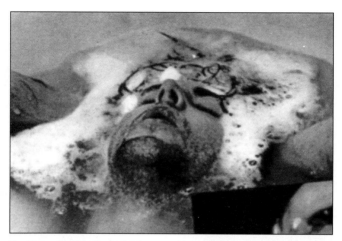

Paul lying back in the bathtub was said to suggest a decapitated corpse.

Are these ghostly, skeletal hands reaching out to claim Paul?

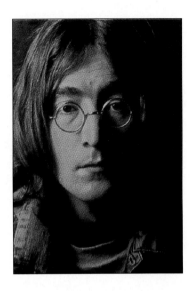

The four individual photos of the Beatles from *The White Album*. Notice that Paul's likeness stands out from the other three. Some investigators claim that if you look closely enough, you can see scars (supposedly from plastic surgery) along Paul's upper lip. Was this the result of the motor bike accident or a clever attempt to disguise a double?

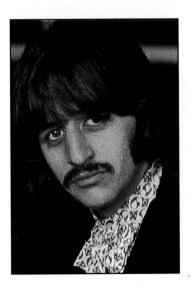

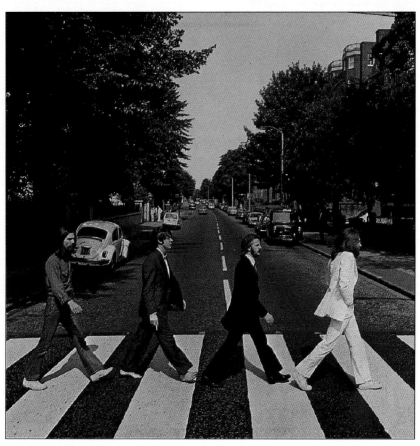

The alleged funeral procession that started the death clue hysteria.

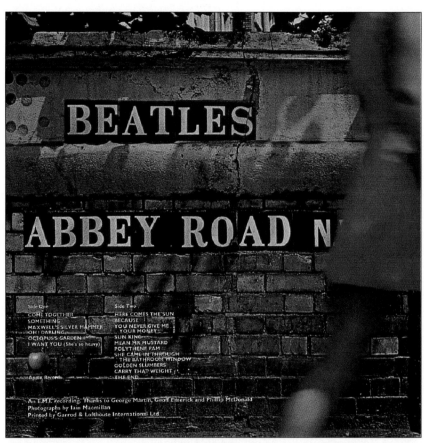

The backside of *Abbey Road* presents a series of dots that appear to form the numeral three. A crack running through the "S" suggests a flaw within the band. A skull made out of shadow and light seems to ominously follow the Beatles' sign upon the wall.

THE CASE OF THE 'MISSING' BEATLE

Paul is still with us

Paul and
his family
last week
in Scotland

The Magical
McCartney
Mystery

NOVEMBER 7 · 1969 · 40¢

The *Life* magazine cover dated November 7, 1969, was meant to reassure readers that Paul was still with us. Surprisingly, this cover held other clues that added fuel to the death-clue hysteria.

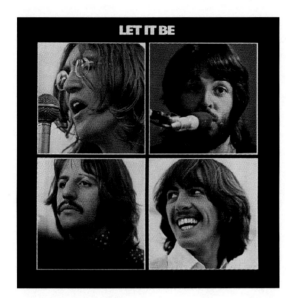

The album cover in funeral black proved to be the Beatles' swan song. Notice that Paul, again, is different from the others. John, George, and Ringo are in profile with a white background while Paul faces the camera with a blood-red background.

Death rumors were also flying with the release of Paul's solo album, *McCartney.* Supposedly, there is an Old English saying, "Life Is A Bowl Of Cherries." In this case, the bowl is empty!

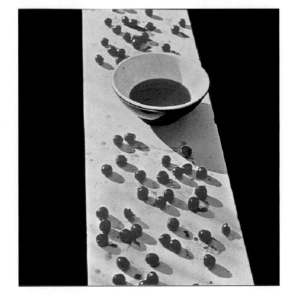

CHAPTER 8

*One And
One And
One Is Three*

"Come Together"

Since the material for the *Let It Be* album sat unused in the studio, the Beatles made plans for what proved to be their swan song LP. Paul McCartney approached George Martin and asked if they could make an album like they had in the past. Martin remembered: "I was really surprised when after we had finished that album [*Let It Be*] Paul came to me and said, 'Let's get back and record like we used to -- would you produce an album like you used to?' 'Well, if you'd allow me to, I will.' And that's how we made *Abbey Road*. It wasn't quite like the old days because they were still working on their own songs. And they would bring in the other people to work as kind of musicians for them rather than being a team" (Dowlding, 273).

Under the guidance of George Martin, the *Abbey Road* LP was recorded quickly and brought back memories of the early excitement the Beatles generated in the pre-*Sgt. Pepper's* recordings. Though the recording magic still lingered, so did the stress that finally ripped the Beatles apart.

The conflict grew between the members of the group but now was much more noticeable between Lennon and McCartney. It seemed that the *Abbey Road* album would be split between the primitive rock and roll songs of John Lennon as opposed to the lush, heavily-produced numbers of Paul McCartney. Martin told *Rolling Stone:* "[the long fifteen minute compilation on side two] was Paul and I getting along together because Paul really dug what I wanted to do. I was trying to make a symphony out of pop music. I was trying to get Paul to write stuff that we could then bring in on counterpoint, or sort of a movement that referred back to something else. Bring some form into the thing. John hated that -- he liked good old rock 'n' roll. *Abbey Road* became another of many compromises.

Side One of the LP was a collection of Lennon's individual songs. John doesn't like tone poems, or whatever you call it" (Schaffner, 124).

McCartney recalled in a *Life* magazine article dated April 16, 1971, "By the time we made *Abbey Road,* John and I were openly critical of each other's music, and I felt John wasn't much interested in performing anything he hadn't written himself." In the October, 1986, issue of *Musician,* Paul continued with an insight dealing with the open friction between the Beatles: "On *Abbey Road* I was beginning to get too producer-y for everyone. George Martin was the actual producer, and I was beginning to be too definite. George [Harrison] and Ringo turned around and said: 'Look, piss off! We're grown-ups and we can do it without you fine.' For people like me who don't really realize when they're being very overbearing, it comes as a great surprise to be told. So I completely clammed up and backed off -- 'right, okay, they're right, I'm a turd.' So a day or two went by and the session started to flag a bit and eventually Ringo turned 'round to me and said: 'Come on. . . produce!' You couldn't have it both ways. You either had to have me doing what I did, which, let's face it, I hadn't done too bad, or I was going to back off and become paranoid myself, which was what happened."

In *Beatle Songs,* William Dowlding referred to another particular incident: "One night during the album's recording, McCartney called Abbey Road to say he wouldn't be coming in to the studio because it was the anniversary of his meeting Linda and they wanted to spend a romantic evening together. This infuriated Lennon, who ran over to McCartney's house at 7 Cavendish Avenue, rushed in, yelled at him for inconveniencing the others, and smashed a painting he had done and given to Paul" (Dowlding, 273).

The *Abbey Road* album also contained a single that was released only to bring in money for Apple Productions. This was done at the insistence of Allen Klein and, surprisingly, the A-side of the 45 belonged to George Harrison's "Something." Lennon later referred to this composition as the best recording on the album. Frank Sinatra went even further by exclaiming that "Something" was "the greatest love song of the past fifty years."

Harrison wrote "Something" for his then wife Patti Boyd Harrison. Patti later inspired Eric Clapton's memorable "Layla" and would eventually become Clapton's wife. In *I Me Mine* Harrison stated: "'Something' was written on the piano while we were making *The White*

Album. I had a break while Paul was doing some overdubbing, so I went into an empty studio and began to write. That's really all there is to it, except the middle took some time to sort out! It didn't go on *The White Album* because we'd already finished all the tracks. I gave it to Joe Cocker a year before I did it. It's probably got a range of five notes which fit most singers' needs best. This I suppose is my most successful song with over 150 cover versions [second only to 'Yesterday']. My favorite version is the one by James Brown -- that was excellent. When I wrote it, in my mind I heard Ray Charles singing it, and he did do it some years later. I like Smokey Robinson's version, too."

The song proved so popular that it was used as a TV commercial for Chrysler LeBaron Coupes in late 1987 and early 1988. This was about the same time that Nike reportedly paid Capitol Records $250,000 to use the Beatle version of "Revolution" in their TV shoe ads. This concept of commercialization was met with mixed opinions. Yoko Ono believed that Nike should use the Beatles' version and that "John's songs should not be part of a cult of glorified martyrdom. They should be enjoyed by kids today."

McCartney stated, "I haven't made up my mind. . .generally, I don't like it, particularly with the Beatles' stuff. When twenty more years have passed, maybe we'll move into the realm where it's okay to do it."

George Harrison also voiced his opinion on the subject: "If it's allowed to happen, every Beatles' song ever recorded is going to be advertising women's underwear and sausages. We've got to put a stop to it in order to set a precedent. Otherwise, it's going to be a free-for-all. . . it's one thing if you're dead, but we're still around! They don't have any respect for the fact that we wrote and recorded those songs, and that it was our lives" (Dowlding, 208-9).

George Harrison bitterly remembered the release of "Something": "They [Lennon and McCartney] blessed me with a couple of B-sides in the past, but this is the first time that I've had an A-side. Big deal!" (Schaffner, 124).

In the *Playboy Interviews,* John Lennon offered this explanation: "'Something' was the first time he ever got an A-side because Paul and I always either wrote both sides anyway. . .not because we were keeping him out. . .simply, his material wasn't up to scratch. That's the reality of it. It wasn't a conspiracy. He just didn't have the material" (Sheff, 147).

The release of *Abbey Road* took place on September 26, 1969, in the United Kingdom, and on October 1, 1969, in the United States. In the United States, the recording entered the album chart at number 178, jumped to number four one week later, and reached number one the following week, where it remained for eleven weeks. It stayed in the top 30 for thirty-one weeks. The total world sales were estimated to be 10 million at the end of 1980 (Dowlding, 272).

Of all the Beatle albums that generated the McCartney death clues, *Abbey Road* proved to be the most sinister. The album jacket contained a photograph taken at Abbey Road at 10 AM on August 8, 1969. In *John Lennon: One Day At A Time*, Anthony Fawcett shared this story behind the album cover's photographs: "Everybody was laughing about the fact that Paul had arrived with no shoes, and even though his house was just around the corner, he said he couldn't be bothered to go get any. McMillan set up his camera in the middle of Abbey Road, right outside the studios, and while the police stopped traffic the Beatles walked across the road three or four times. He kept shouting: 'Stop! Start Again,' until he was confident that he had the right shot. Happy with the front cover, McMillan asked me [Fawcett] to drive with him along Abbey Road to look for the best street sign to photograph for the back cover. It had to be one of the old-style tiled signs set into the bricks. The best one was at the far end of Abbey Road, and we set up the camera on the edge of the pavement. McMillan decided to take a series of shots and was angry when, in the middle of them, a girl in a blue dress walked by, oblivious to what was happening. But this turned out to be the most interesting shot, and the Beatles [led by Paul McCartney] chose it for the back cover. Afterward, I joined John and Yoko at Paul's house in St. John's Wood, where everybody had gone for tea after the photo session."

The album photographs meant much more to the legions of Beatle mystery sleuths who searched painstakingly for clues to McCartney's death. The four Beatles walking precisely across the street was thought to have symbolized a funeral procession. Since John Lennon was dressed completely in white, he was said to have represented the church, or even the Deity -- white, of course being the traditional color of mourning in many Eastern cultures. Ringo, who was next in the procession and dressed neatly in black, represented the undertaker, or better yet, the priest who respectfully followed Lennon's Deity. Paul McCartney followed behind Ringo and was barefoot with his eyes closed. In a number of societies corpses are buried without their shoes. Again, many assumed that this figure was the great Beatle impostor.

This Paul held a cigarette in his right hand when every true Beatle fan knew that the real McCartney was left-handed! The McCartney look-alike was also out of step with the other three Beatles. John, Ringo, and George were in perfect step. Each led with his left foot, while McCartney led with his right foot.

McCartney remembered the photo scene in a *Rolling Stone* interview in 1973: "It was a hot day in London, a really nice hot day -- barefoot, nice warm day, I didn't feel like wearing shoes. So I went around to the photo session and showed me bare feet. . .turns out to be some old Mafia sign of death or something."

This would be very convincing. However, in the *Magical Mystery Tour* LP Paul appears in two other scenes barefoot. In one scene, his empty shoes stand next to Ringo's drum kit and appear to be covered in blood. George Harrison, dressed in work clothes, was the last of the group in the procession and, to many, represented the gravedigger.

Equally puzzling is Paul McCartney's explanation for why he chose not to wear shoes: "a hot day in London." Everyone knows that on hot days, asphalt becomes unbearably hot. Surely, then, McCartney would have realized his dilemma when faced with the photograph session and the infamous walk across Abbey Road.

One of the most puzzling explanations to this scene is why the Beatles chose to walk across the street from West to East. Since there are song references to the sun on *Abbey Road* (e.g., "Here Comes The Sun" and "Sun King"), the Beatles may have referred to the sun's cycle and related this to a comparison of the human life span. In ancient societies, Egypt in particular, the dead were buried facing west. In Egypt, early Pharaohs were enshrined in their houses of eternity on the western side of the Nile river. This would be in accordance to the end-cycle of the sun as it sets in the West. Of course, it is tradition in Christian societies that corpses are buried facing eastward. This, perchance, represented the glorious rising of the dead which followed the teachings of the Christian Rapture. If the Beatles symbolically represented a burial scene, it would then appear that the group should walk from East to West and represent the earthly cycle of birth to death. The visual clues now suggested that the album photograph did not represent a burial but instead, a resurrection. This resurrection followed the direction of the sun cycle in which the sun appeared in the East, in this case, denoting a new birth. This followed the Eastern concept of the rebirth of Krishna, which generated this new era of wisdom and love. The public today is well aware of the religious concept of being born-again.

If one looked over the inside shoulder of George Harrison, an eerie message is shown on the license plate of the parked Volkswagen Beetle. The license plate reads "LMW 28IF." The "28IF" represented the age of the true Paul McCartney. In this case, McCartney would have been 28 if he were alive. It didn't seem to make much difference that Paul was actually twenty-seven years of age when *Abbey Road* was released.

The cynics countered that in Far Eastern societies an individual's birth included the time spent in the mother's womb. In this case, Paul McCartney would indeed have been twenty-eight. According to McCartney in a February, 1988, *Musician* interview: "That Volkswagen has just recently been sold for a fortune. But it meant nothing you know."

Actually, according to Mark Lewisohn's *The Beatles: Recording Sessions*, the Volkswagen sold for 2,300 pounds at a Sotheby's auction in 1986. Louis Yager actually placed a phone call to the owner of the Volkswagen. He accomplished this by going through automobile registration records and placing an overseas call to a London number, rather late one night, awakened an elderly lady who simply and mysteriously "declined comment" (*Life,* November 7, 1969).

It would be in dramatic grim irony to have a Volkswagen Beetle serve as conclusion to the tombstone introduced on the *Sgt. Pepper's* drum head. In this case, the age of the deceased Beetle, or Beatle, now completed the full epitaph. With the drum skin message, we learn who died and the date of the death. The Volkswagen gives us the age of the individual and helps complete the cycle that began with *Sgt. Pepper's.*

On the back side of the *Abbey Road* album cover is Fawcett's grimly-shadowed stone wall. The picture contained a montage of light and shadow. A sign that reads "Beatles" is displayed prominently against the wall in large block letters. Each letter was perfectly formed except for the letter 'S.' There is a small, rather minute, jagged crack, running through the imperfect letter. This possibly hinted at a flaw within what was once thought to be the perfect rock-n-roll band.

The use of this flaw brought forth references of Samuel Taylor Coleridge's "Christabel" and John Keats' "Lamia." Coleridge's Geraldine from "Christabel" and Keats' Lamia were examples of supernatural creatures who assumed any shapes desired. This shape appeared perfect at first glance, but upon closer examination, a slight deformity was evident.

In Shakespeare's *Macbeth*, (1.3) one of the witches mentioned taking the shape of "a rat without a tail" or, in the case of Geraldine, a beautiful woman with a withered breast. The use of this age-old legend allowed the Beatles to point to an impostor as they staged visual clues that now hinted at a flaw.

Examples of these imperfections included the hand over McCartney's head and his back turned to the camera from *Sgt. Pepper's Lonely Hearts Club Band;* Paul dressed in military dress and the black carnation he wore from *Magical Mystery Tour;* Paul's close-up photograph from *The White Album;* and the mysterious funeral procession from *Abbey Road.*

The back side of *Abbey Road* contained other death clues. To the immediate left of "Beatles" etched into stone, a series of dots appeared to be machine-gunned haphazardly against the wall. If the dots are connected in the fashion of the popular children's game of "Connect the Dots," one can easily make out the number "3." After the number three becomes visible, the complete sign would then read "3 Beatles." But everyone knew that there were four Beatles, and that on the front of *Abbey Road,* the four members were pictured walking across the street; but what if the clue meant that of the four, only three were original members? One, then, must surely be a replacement or impostor. This fit perfectly with the "Paul Is Dead" hysteria.

One of the most intriguing questions concerned the girl in the blue dress who just happened to pass by at the time of the photograph. Many investigators concluded that the girl was none other than Jane Asher, the one-time fiancée of McCartney. Of course this could be another example of a fertile imagination at work, but Jane Asher was a model, and a great number of Beatle fans, at this time, refused to accept Paul's marriage to Linda Eastman.

In the recordings on *Abbey Road,* there are also clues that reinforced the death theory. The first song of side one is a John Lennon-influenced rocker entitled "Come Together." In *The Playboy Interviews* Lennon stated, "'Come Together' is me -- writing obscurely around an old Chuck Berry thing. I left the line in 'Here comes old flat-top.' It is nothing like the Chuck Berry song, but they took me to court because I admitted the influence once years ago. I could have changed it to

----

'Here comes old iron face,' but the song remains independent of Chuck Berry or anybody else on Earth. The thing was created in the studio. It's gobbledygook; 'Come Together' was an expression that Tim Leary had come up with for his attempt at being president or whatever he wanted to be, [actually, Leary had come up with the idea of running against Ronald Reagan for the office of governor of California] and he asked me to write a campaign song. I tried and I tried, but I couldn't come up with one. But I came up with this, 'Come Together,' which would've been no good to him -- you couldn't have a campaign song like that, right? Leary attacked me years later, saying I ripped him off. I didn't rip him off. It's just that it turned into 'Come Together.' What am I going to do, give it to him? It was a funky record -- it's one of my favorite Beatle tracks, or, one of my favorite Lennon tracks. Let's say that. It's funky, it's bluesy, and I'm singing it pretty well. I like the sound of the record. You can dance to it. I'll buy it!" (Scheff, 179).

Actually, the Chuck Berry song was entitled "You Can't Catch Me" and Lennon settled by performing "You Can't Catch Me" and "Sweet Little Sixteen" on his *Rock and Roll* album in 1975 and "Ya Ya" on the *Wall and Bridges* LP in 1974. What these three numbers have in common is that the songs are owned by Big Seven Music, a company that benefited financially by Lennon's re-recording these selections from their catalog.

The lyric content of "Come Together" contained some references that helped convince Beatle listeners that an underlying tragedy was hidden beneath the lyrics. The first verse started with the line "Here comes old flat top," which many sleuths suggested was a reference to a headless body. The same verse mentioned that the mysterious "he" had "hair down to his knee." John Lennon was into Hair Peace and Bagism, as evidenced in the line "Bag production," but again, many observers interpreted this line as the superstition that in death, a corpse's hair continues to grow. The last line of the first verse mentioned a reference to "Got to be a joker, he just do what he please." This line strongly hinted at the idea of a hoax. Was McCartney the joker who did as he pleased? In this case, could Paul have managed to pull off the greatest hoax in music history? The line "He wear no shoe shine" may refer to the barefoot McCartney walking across the cover of *Abbey Road.*

There are other examples of standard Beatle humor on the album. "I Want You (She's So Heavy)" ended abruptly in mid-bar progression, and the second side of the *Abbey Road* LP ended with a tongue-in-cheek

----

composition entitled "Her Majesty," which was not mentioned on the play list.

The "Come Together" chorus, "Come together, right now, over me," suggested a return to the *Sgt. Pepper's* album cover. Again the observer is reminded of the wake scene in which "a crowd of people stood and stared" at the flower-decorated grave of the fallen Beatle. Were these people, as well as the surviving members of the Beatles, coming together as mourners at the funeral service?

The phrase "over me" perhaps referred to the corpse that rested peacefully in his grave as the onlookers paid their last respects by gazing at his grave.

Later in the third verse, the line "Walrus gambols" is mentioned. This alluded to the earlier references of the walrus symbol. Possibly the most intriguing line was found in the fourth verse. The phrase "He say one and one and one is three" referred to the back side of the *Abbey Road* album cover and brought to mind the mysterious dots that, when connected, formed the number three; in this case, another reference to the number three, or the three surviving Beatles.

The next line "Got to be good-looking 'cause he's so hard to see" brought to mind images of Paul, "the cute Beatle," who may very well have been too hard to see in the shadowy netherworld of death.

CHAPTER 9

Number Nine?
Number Nine?
"Revolution 9"

The *Life* Magazine Article
of November 7, 1969,
and Paul's Reply?

When radio station WKNR-FM lit up the airways with the grim news of the death rumors in October, 1969, the public demanded to know the truth: If Paul McCartney were not dead, then where was he? The other Beatles either refused to comment, except for Ringo who called the rumors "a load of old crap." Ringo related that John Lennon was dressed in the black walrus suit on the cover of *Magical Mystery Tour* -- not Paul McCartney.

The rumors continued. "One day following the sounds of Martha's [Paul's sheep dog] barking, Paul found himself facing a full complement of *Life* magazine reporters and photographers, dispatched by the publication to verify the official statement made so many times a day by Derek Taylor that Paul was not in the hereafter but only in Scotland. Paul's response to this intrusion upon his privacy was to heave a pail of water over the nearest *Life* photographer. Fleeing the unexpected, but most certainly corporeal wrath of their subject, the *Life* team descended to Campbelltown. In hot pursuit in his Land-Rover came Paul McCartney, miraculously transformed into the PR man who had always broken the ice with the press and offered them cups of tea. In exchange for the film of his uncharacteristic display of fury, Paul offered a full interview with exclusive Linda McCartney pictures of himself and his new baby. 'Rumors of my death have been greatly exaggerated,' he told the magazine. 'However, if I was dead, I'm sure I'd be the last to know'" (Salewicz, 222).

Life magazine offered this account: "*Life* London Correspondent Dorothy Bacon waded through a bog in Scotland to reach Paul McCartney's secluded farm and get this comment from him: 'It is all bloody stupid. I picked up that OPD badge in Canada. It was a police badge. Perhaps it means Ontario Police Department or something. I was

----

wearing a black flower because they ran out of red ones. It is John, not me, dressed in black on the cover and inside of *Magical Mystery Tour.* On *Abbey Road* we were wearing our ordinary clothes. I was walking barefoot because it was a hot day. The Volkswagen just happened to be parked there. Perhaps the rumor started because I haven't been much in the press lately. I have done enough press for a lifetime and I don't have anything to say these days. I am happy to be with my family and I will work when I work. I was switched on for 10 years and I never switched off. Now I am switching off whenever I can. I would rather be less famous these days. I would rather do what I began by doing, which was making music. We make good music and we want to go on making good music. But the Beatle thing is over. It has exploded, partly by what we have done and partly by other people. We are individuals, all different. John married Yoko, I married Linda. We didn't marry the same girl. The people who are making up these rumors should look to themselves a little more. There is not enough time in life. They should worry about themselves instead of worrying whether I am dead or not. What I have to say is all in the music. If I want to say anything I write a song. Can you spread it around that I am just an ordinary person and want to live in peace? We have to go now, we have two children at home'" (*Life,* November 7, 1969).

McCartney recalled later in a radio interview that someone at Apple asked what they were to do when American disc jockeys spread the word of Paul's tragic accident. McCartney replied, "Sounds like good publicity to me. Tell them I'm not." Of course, this response took weeks to reach the media. This gave the public plenty of time to buy Beatle albums and search for clues.

Almost incredulously, the photo of McCartney accompanying the magazine article suggested another clue to Paul's demise. The back side of the magazine cover, which depicted McCartney and his family with the glad tidings that "Paul Is Still With Us," contained an advertisement for an automobile. If the cover photograph is held up to the light, the automobile is seen across McCartney's chest blocking out his body. Paul's head is the only discernible image that breaks through the black void. This is yet another eerie coincidence pointing towards McCartney's having been decapitated in the automobile accident.

The Beatles, as a group, ebbed slowly following the release of *Abbey Road.* The long-awaited Phil Spector production of *Let It Be* was finally ready for release and now served as the grand finale for the world's

----

greatest rock and roll band. Unfortunately, the Beatles still squabbled over which should be released first -- *Let It Be* or Paul McCartney's solo album, simply titled *McCartney*. Paul refused to allow his album to wait until after the *Let It Be* release. In hopes of changing Paul's mind, Ringo was sent by the others to help solve the release problem.

In Peter McCabe and Robert D. Schonfeld's *Apple To The Core*, the authors contained Ringo's account of the visit: "To my [Ringo's] dismay, he [Paul] went completely out of control, shouting at me, prodding his fingers toward my face, saying, 'I'll finish you all now' and 'you'll pay.' He told me to put my coat on and get out. . .while I thought he had behaved a bit like a spoiled child, I could see that the release of his record had a gigantic emotional significance for him. . .and I felt. . .we should let him have his own way."

McCartney did indeed have his way, and *McCartney* was released in April, 1970. To many investigators, even this solo LP held a death clue. The cover depicted an empty bowl of cherries. Could this refer to the saying, "Life is a bowl of cherries?" Only in this case the bowl was empty!

Along with this release, Paul made it official -- he was no longer a Beatle. McCartney's surprise announcement infuriated John Lennon. Lennon felt that he should have left the group earlier, and that Paul had managed to trick him into staying a Beatle much longer than he had originally wanted. John referred to the making of *Let It Be* as "hell. . .it was the most miserable session on earth" (*Rolling Stone*, September 11, 1986).

George Harrison's comments echoed Lennon's statement: "I couldn't stand it! I decided, this is it! It's just not fun anymore; as a matter of fact, it's very unhappy being in this band at all" (*The Beatles: A Celebration*).

Paul, however, went for the jugular. At his press conference, his official statement stated that his break from the Beatles was "due to personal differences, musical differences, business differences, but most of all because I have a better time with my family" (Schaffner, 135). Paul also included a few more digs at his fellow bandmates:

Q: *Will Paul and Linda become a John and Yoko?*

A: No, they will become a Paul and Linda.

Q: *Do you miss the other Beatles and George Martin?*
Was there a moment, e.g., when you thought "Wish
Ringo was here for this break?"

A: No.

Q: *Do you foresee a time when Lennon-McCartney*
becomes an active songwriting partnership again?

A: No.

Q: *What do you feel about John's peace effort? The*
Plastic Ono Band? Yoko?

A: I love John and respect what he does, but it
doesn't give me any pleasure.

Q: *What is your relationship with Klein?*

A: It isn't. And he doesn't represent me in any
way.

It now appeared that the *Let It Be* LP was suitably designed in funeral black. The color may not have only insinuated Paul's death, but also served as the obituary for the fab-foursome. Other death clues from the *Let It Be* album included Paul's looking directly into the camera lens while the other Beatles present their left profiles.

Each of the three Beatles in profile have a white background, whereas McCartney's background is blood red! In December of 1969, *The Beatles Monthly* (the major fan magazine for the Beatles) ended after 77 issues. The magazine had been in existence before the release of "She Loves You." In parting, the fan magazine took these parting shots at the individual Beatle members: "The Beatles were denounced for having grown uncooperative about posing for photographs; for having failed to come out against drugs; for having lost their sense of humor ['Everything seems to be very, very serious. Nothing is just plain fun anymore.']; and even for their appearance ['The Beatles are certainly tremendously

----

photogenic, or at least they were in the days when you could see all of their faces']" (Schaffner, 131).

The Beatles now pursued solo careers, but were not always as successful as they may have imagined. Ringo released *Sentimental Journey* (originally entitled *Ringo Stardust)* in 1970 and dedicated it to his mother. The selections included "Love Is A Many Splendored Thing" and showcased the big band era. The critical reaction to this album was simply embarrassed silence. Ringo later went to Nashville, Tennessee, and recorded his *Beaucoup of Blues* LP with Pete Drake and other Nashville session players. It was obvious that the former Beatle had a fondness for country music (e.g., "Act Naturally").

When the single "Back Off Boogaloo" was released in March, 1972, the normally-calm and peaceful Ringo lashed out at a mysterious meathead in these lines: "Wake up meathead, don't forget that you were dead." Was this meathead Paul McCartney? Was this an attempt to confirm the public's suspicions of the great death hoax? Ringo, John, and George often used the code-name "Boogaloo" to secretly refer to McCartney. In one instance Starr remarked that he had "Boogaloo on the phone."

It seemed appropriate that Ringo released *It Don't Come Easy* earlier in 1971, and this effort, for once, towered above Lennon's *Power To The People,* McCartney's *Another Day* and Harrison's *Bangla Desh.* It seemed that Ringo stood out from his more prolific songwriting partners and was finally allowed his place in the spotlight.

John Lennon released his signature LP *Imagine* in October, 1971. The album contained "How Do You Sleep?" an attack on Paul McCartney. "In case any listener missed the object of his scorn, a postcard was included with *Imagine* that showed Lennon in a delicious parody of McCartney's *Ram* album cover. 'Those freaks was right when they said you was dead' sang Lennon in a vicious put-down. He was referring to bizarre rumors, particularly in America, that Paul McCartney was, in fact, dead" (Coleman, 462). Some later critics claim that Lennon referred only to his concept of McCartney's decline as a writer.

Although George Harrison did not attack McCartney directly at this time (he would later attack both Lennon and McCartney) he did take part in the production of both songs. He played the guitar lines for each composition and joined in the role as a fellow conspirator.

The search for an explanation to the death clues continued. The Beatles only stated that there was no attempt on their part to mislead the public. In the *Playboy Interviews* (1980), David Sheff asked Lennon: "Were you amused by the 'Paul Is Dead' thing when everyone was playing your records backward and crying?"

John responded, "They all had a good time. It was meaningless" (Sheff, 81).

From a *Rolling Stone* interview dated January 7, 1971, the interviewer asked John: "Were any of those things really on the albums that were said to be there? The clues?" to which Lennon responded: "No. That was bullshit, the whole thing was made up. We did put in 'tit, tit, tit' in 'Girl.'"

Despite Lennon's public denial of the rumors, the conspiracy theories of Paul's death continued to grow. Joel Glazier, a college professor, used to electrify Beatle conventions with his presentation of the death clues. His scenarios included a belief that the CIA was responsible for Paul's death in an attempt to rid the world of Beatle influences. This same theory has recently been used to draw John Lennon's assassination into the covert wing of the CIA. When Glazier was questioned by younger McCartney fans who had witnessed the former Beatle in concert, the professor responded, "I've never given any thought to whether Paul really died or not. I've been too busy looking for clues ever since" (Schaffner, 129).

In the early days of the death rumors, Lewis Yager called Alex Bennett's talk show and "claimed to have been awakened in the night by the screams of a Beatlemaniacal girlfriend to whom McCartney's dire fate had been revealed in a dream." Yager later made this statement: "Everyone knows it was a hoax. But people still love hearing the clues. It was the most fascinating stunt in years" (Schaffner, 129).

Sociologist Barbara Suczek, in her essay "The Curious Death of Paul McCartney," interviewed typical thirteen and fourteen-year olds and recorded their feelings that related to the death clues. The young fans' responses? "It makes me feel all tingly!"; "Dark! It's a very dark feeling. I don't know how else to tell you"; "It's mysterious and creepy. Sometimes it's depressing"; "You're hooked into something -- something strange."

It seemed that grim irony continued to follow the Beatles after their break-up. The senseless murder of John Lennon on December 8, 1980, in New York City brought back memories of previously-released

---

Beatle material such as the album *Revolver* (John was killed with a handgun), and the Beatle song "Happiness is a Warm Gun," which many investigators believed hinted at Lennon's possible use of heroin.

The most bizarre reference to John's death is contained in the opening lyric line to "Come Together." John's vocal mutterings exclaimed "Shoot me." The "me" is hidden behind the first notes of the bass guitar line.

In a bizarre twist of irony, John and Yoko lived in the Dakota apartment complex in New York, which served as the site for Roman Polanski's *Rosemary's Baby* a film based upon Satanism and the occult. Strangely, during the *Playboy Interviews*, John heard a scream from outside and stated, "Oh, another murder at rue Dakota (laughter)" (Scheff, 91). The list of Lennon coincidences helped provide a chilling retrospect to the "Paul Is Dead" rumors.

The field of psychology also became extremely interested in the McCartney death rumors. A 1976 tome titled *Rumor and Gossip: The Social Psychology of Hearsay*, by Ralph Rosnow and Gary Fine, featured an extensive passage on the McCartney hoax, which the authors also explored in the August, 1974, issue of *Human Behavior.* The two psychologists concluded that, like most rumors, this one was spread as an unconscious attempt on the part of rumormongers to gain status in exchange for precious information. Yet "it had markings of a budding legend or literary invention, rather than the news item it supposedly was. The clearest function of this rumor. . .was its entertainment value. It was fun hunting for clues and talking about the mystery with friends. The rumor flourished for many of the same reasons that mystery stories are so popular -- suspense without fear and emotional stimulation."

That some people were willing to believe the rumor, according to Drs. Rosnow and Fine "implies that the world and in particular the mass media are deceptive. This generation had been brought up on the Kennedy assassination and the considerable doubt focused on the Warren Commission Report. The credibility gap of Lyndon Johnson's Presidency, the widely circulated rumors after the Martin Luther King, Jr., and Robert Kennedy assassinations, as well as attacks on the leading media sources by the Yippies and Spiro Agnew, no doubt helped to foster an attitude in which a mass conspiracy was not out of the question. A person, one of world renown, could be replaced by another for three years in the eyes of this audience without anyone being the wiser" (Schaffner, 128).

The human race, it seems, has always been obsessed with the macabre. Stephen King's novels take us by the hand and lead us into the darkest recesses of our hidden fears. Of course, we have to look into the void. We cannot hide our eyes, cry under the covers and scream for our mother's assurance that it is only a dream. In this case, we, as a race, are fascinated by our own morality.

The "creepy" and "tingly" feelings described by the fourteen-year olds in Barbara Suczek's study confirmed that we each have primeval fears that have existed since the dawn of time. In 1945, a series of rumors concerning the death of Franklin Delano Roosevelt swept the nation: "Newspapers, radio stations, banks, and even corner drugstores were deluged with calls asking if it were true that this, that, or the other person had died, or been killed in an accident" (Jacobson, 460).

While theories of hidden conspiracy and intrigue have been proven for the most part to be groundless, there is still that remote chance that a researcher may stumble upon the one elusive gem of wisdom that will bring forth new evidence and solve the hidden mysteries of the past and lead the way to a better understanding of those significant figures who helped shape our history, our culture, and our very lives.

Throughout our literary history, man has written tales of heroes and gods. In certain instances heroes are reborn to be worshipped as gods, as in the case of Alexander the Great. This premise may have been the catalyst behind the entire Beatle death theory. The rumors became elements of the traditional epic. The scops (storytellers) were the rumor-seekers who sang their songs to the mesmerized multitudes. The clues were passed down by word of mouth to preserve the life line between fact and legend.

In the November 2, 1969, issue of the *New York Times,* J. Marks noted: "The death and resurrection of heroes appears to be as important to the generation that worships rock as it is to the tribes that celebrate the demise and return of various vegetable gods. Whether the McCartney death is purely physical or metaphorical or even metaphysical, it is probable that there is more than a little of the mythic logic of the Cambridge school of classical anthropology involved. No one believes in anything any more and man has a deep need to believe. Remove his objects of belief and he will create others."

In "The Curious Case of the Death of Paul McCartney," sociologist Barbara Suczek lists five specific points dealing with an explanation of the McCartney mystery as to how the cryptic clues ascended to the realm of legend:

(1) This content was relatively stable, lacking the ongoing, developmental quality that usually characterizes a news story. Among its believers, the story was taught and learned, deviations from the theme were definitively discouraged, and the fundamental details were memorized like a litany.

In this case new learners were instructed by the masters as to the relevance of the death clues. Only one interpretation seemed justified. All deviations or questions as to the accepted validity of the precepts were frowned upon. The cryptic clues became as inherent to the new-found faith as the Masonic creed or the granting of the mystic goodies during a fraternity initiation. The secret interpretations were fostered in silence and taught to new initiates verbally. These initiates thus became the next generation of neophytes, binding themselves through their new found allegiance to the perpetuation of the new-grown legend.

(2) The story shared with the legend a quality of empirical irrelevance. To whom, after all, but a few academicians, does it matter if legendary heroes actually lived and did the deeds attributed to them? The significance of the story transcends the details of individual biography. The fact, or lack of it, of the death of Paul McCartney seemed similarly irrelevant to its publics. The inference, then, is that the Paul McCartney of this story was a symbol, a social construct that no longer required facts of a personal existence to sustain it.

(3) An almost Gothic engrossment with death and the occult permeated virtually every aspect of the phenomenon -- twin themes that are fundamental to myth.

(4) The content of the story recalls the pattern that categorically defines a cyclical myth. The untimely death of a beautiful youth who is subsequently transformed into or revealed to be a god is a recurrent mythical theme and is presumed to reflect the cyclical process in nature.

The legends of Osirius, Adonis, Dionysus, and Jesus have all conformed, in some major way, to this pattern. It may be the McCartney rumor represents an aborted attempt to re-create such a myth. Perhaps in the present, as in the past, humans may be trying to make sense out of the apparent senselessness of their own deaths by suggesting, analogously, the possibility of reincarnation. Alternately, such a myth may be a process whereby socially valued qualities of an exemplary youth can be abstracted into an idealized model and thus be preserved from the eroding onslaughts of ongoing reality (a motivation described by Wallace Stevens as 'nostalgia for perfection').

(5) Clearly the rumor had high entertainment value. Not only did it provide a fascinating subject for conversation, but it also invoked -- particularly among younger adolescents -- a fearful, brooding, supernatural mood which they obviously found rather more enjoyable than otherwise. The entertainment component is an important factor in the promulgation of a myth since the pleasure of its company makes its repetition a likelihood.

The so-called McCartney myth relates to one of the more memorable legends in English literature, that of the Fisher King. According to Gertrude Jobes' *Dictionary of Mythology, Folklore, and Symbols,* the Fisher King is the archetype for a "king whose virility is tied to the fertility of the land. If he ages, becomes ill, is wounded, or turns sexually impotent, his sterility causes the land to waste; his restoration brings verdure back to the land. A fertility or vegetation god -- in Grail romances custodian of Grail castle, possessor of the bleeding lance, the Grail, and the silver plate. Maimed by a spear thrust through his thigh, he found solace in fishing. He can be healed only by a Grail-seeker; when he is healed the waste land which surrounds his castle will become fertile once again."

The Grail is a literary, as well as Christian symbol that relates to the cup that Christ drank from at the Last Supper. The same cup, according to legend and Webster's, was used by Joseph of Arimathea to collect Christ's spilled blood during the Crucifixion. The quest for this miraculous cup has been a source of inspiration from Sir Thomas Mallory's *Le Morte d'Arthur* to Steven Spielberg's *Indiana Jones and the Last Crusade.*

The Beatles themselves could have filled the symbolic role of the Fisher King. In 1967, Lennon was convinced that the older Beatle material had become a "wasteland" of thought. With this in mind, the Beatles opened new dimensions in thought and sound with the introduction of the *Sgt. Pepper's Lonely Hearts Club Band* LP. The public readily accepted the new sounds and musical direction of the Beatles vision. However, the creative period of *Sgt. Pepper's* was short-lived. The Beatles once again sank into the dismal wasteland of disillusionment. The group argued amongst themselves. Their music became sterile and led to the disunion of the band.

The radical sounds of "Revolution 9" served as an attempt to lead the rock visionaries into even more unexplored realms of sound. As the Beatles withdrew from the public eye, the magical world of rock and roll became unfruitful. The cryptic clues associated with the album covers and song lyrics became the challenge for a new quest -- quest that would return the creative sounds to the long silent songsmiths. Perhaps the music world is waiting for the seeker of the Grail who will once again lead the music world into yet another golden Renaissance of sound.

Unfortunately, in today's musical marketplace most groups are prepared to look the same and sound the same. There is no deviation from what has become the accepted norms of appearance and performance, and so the land grows barren and waits for the new possessor of the magical sounds that will free yet another generation from complacent mediocrity.

The Fisher King symbol is apparent on the *Sergeant Pepper's Lonely Hearts Club Band* LP cover. The cycle of birth, death, and rebirth is evidenced through visual clues. The waxwork figures of the Beatles represent the birth of the band. The members are posed in look-alike outfits and stand above their own grave. The symbolic death of the Beatles is portrayed by the freshly dug grave complete with the funeral arrangements. The rebirth symbol is found in the *Sgt. Pepper's* era -- Beatles dressed in their psychedelic finery. The Beatles had now become the beautiful butterflies released from the imprisoning cocoon of social mores. The birth, death, and rebirth cycle has turned full circle.

The Hindu concept of Siva, Brahma, and Vishnu may be perceived as well. Siva is the power of creation and destruction as evidenced in the cycle of birth, death, and rebirth, while Brahma represents the power of the mind and serves as creator of the world, and Vishnu represents salvation and offers protection for man against evil. In his tenth incarnation, Vishnu will destroy the earth and end the cycle of birth, death, and rebirth for all time as witnessed by the Hindu faith.

James Joyce and T.S. Eliot were both influenced by the Fisher King legends and the cycle of birth, death, and rebirth. One of Joyce's concepts in *Finnegan's Wake* was presenting a cyclical theory of history. This theory was first presented in 1725 by the Italian philosopher Giambattista Vico. Vico wrote that history passed through four phases:

(1) The divine or theocratic in which man was governed by his belief and acceptance of the supernatural. In this state the worship of fertility gods explained the changing of the seasons and was represented in the coming of winter. Legends have existed throughout history that used the belief that a god's death directly brought about the hardships of the winter season. When the climate turned warmer and life began anew, the old god was said to have been reborn. Man's acceptance of this cycle developed his faith and in return, led to the development of religion itself.

(2) The aristocratic stage is represented in the Heroic Age of Homer and in the development of the traditional epics. The great kings and mighty warriors who would govern mankind wisely.

(3) The democratic and individualistic stage is the complete absence of heroes and with mankind sharing in self-rule. In this stage mankind stagnates into a wasteland society and awaits the final stage of history.

(4) The final stage of chaos is represented by man's fall into confusion. With nothing more to believe in, man will again turn to supernatural reference and the cycle will begin anew.

James Joyce, William Butler Yeats, and T.S. Eliot were convinced that their generation was in this final stage of chaos awaiting the sudden shock that would start the process all over again. T.S. Eliot's *Wasteland* conforms to this premise. In Eliot's *The Hollow Men*, the human race becomes blind both spiritually and physically and is unable and unworthy to complete the quest for salvation.

Surprisingly, the Beatle death clues had followed the metaphysical direction of Joyce, Yeats, and Eliot. Their existence as a group bore a resemblance to Vico's statement of history. At first, some individuals referred to the Beatles as supernatural deities. The blind, sick, and crippled reached out to touch the group in search of a miracle. The Beatles became legends overnight.

When the death clues first emerged, adoring fans spread any news of the tragic fate of McCartney to other believers in much the same way as the news of John Kennedy's assassination. In this way the Beatles became the epic heroes for a twentieth century audience.

The Beatles underwent Vico's democratic and individualistic phase after the death of Brian Epstein. The Beatles ruled themselves, though not very successfully, and underwent a glorious evolution into four talented individuals who could no longer fit the demands of a group. The Beatles, now locked in chaos, awaited the final stage; the shock that would start the endless cycle once again.

Vico sincerely believed that a shift through these historic stages would be preceded by a deafening crash of thunder. In Joyce's *Finnegan's Wake*, there are instances of long multi-syllabic terms included to duplicate Vico's thunder crash. For instance, Joyce includes this description at the very beginning of his masterpiece: "The fall (bababadalgharaghtakamminarronnkonnbronntonnerronntuonnthunntrovar rhounawnskawntoohoohoordenenthurnuk!)"

This thunder-like phrase suggested a shift through one of Vico's four stages of history. Since the Beatles, especially McCartney, considered *Sgt. Pepper's Lonely Hearts Club Band* the forerunner of a new age in music, it would be appropriate for them to end the album with their own thunderous crash to signal the birth of a new age.

In *It Was Twenty Years Ago Today,* Derek Taylor described the orchestral crescendo at the conclusion of "A Day In The Life": "The final bunched chords came from all four Beatles and George Martin in the studio, playing three pianos. All of them hit the chords simultaneously, as hard as possible, with the engineer pushing the volume faders way down at the moment of impact. Then, as the noise gradually diminished, the faders were pushed slowly up to top. It took forty-five seconds, and it was done three or four times, piling on a huge sound -- one piano after another, all doing the same thing." This reverberating E Major chord concludes the *Sgt. Pepper's Lonely Hearts Club Band* album and, like a burst of thunder, propels the listener into a new age of musical history.

"Legends persist because. . .they provide answers to the persistent riddles of life. . .they are especially resistant to change" (Allport and Postman, 164). "Myths are religious recitations conceived as symbolic of the play of eternity in time. . .Myths and legends may furnish entertainment incidentally, but they are essentially tutorial" (Campbell, 16).

In David Sheff's *The Playboy Interviews With John Lennon And Yoko Ono*, this question was asked to John Lennon:

Playboy: "Then your purpose is to do more than entertain. The hope that the record will be inspiring and will move people to feel or act differently -- which is just what people want from you: some prescription for life. Is this more responsibility than you would choose to have?"

Lennon: [emphatically]: "No. No, because it's the same bit about saying the Beatles led the sixties. It's not true. The idea of leadership is a false god. If you want to use the Beatles or John and Yoko or whoever, people are expecting them to do something for them. That's not what's going to happen. But they are the ones who didn't understand any message that came before anyway. And they are the ones that will follow Hitler or follow Reverend Moon or whoever. Following is not what it's about, but leaving messages of 'This is what's happening to us. Hey, what's happening to you?'"

Playboy: "What is the eighties dream to you, John?"

Lennon: "Well, you make your own dream. That's the Beatles story isn't it? That's Yoko's story. That's what I'm saying now. Produce your own dream. If you want to save Peru, go save Peru. It's quite possible to do anything, but not if you put it on the leaders and the parking meters. Don't expect Carter or Reagan or John Lennon or Yoko Ono or Bob Dylan or Jesus Christ to come and do it for you. You have to do it yourself. That's what the great masters and mistresses have been saying ever since time began. They can point the way, leave signposts and little instructions in various books that are now called holy and worshipped for the cover of the book and not what it says, but the instructions are all there for all to see, have always been and always will be. There's nothing new under the sun. All the roads lead to Rome. And people cannot provide it for you. I can't wake you up. You can wake you up. I can't cure you. You can cure you."

Playboy: "What is it that keeps people from accepting that message?"

Lennon: "It's fear of the unknown. The unknown is what it is. And to be frightened of it is what sends everybody scurrying around in circles chasing dreams, illusions, wars, peace, love, hate, all that -- it's all an illusion. Unknown is what it is. Accept that it's unknown and it's plain sailing. Everything is unknown -- then you're ahead of the game. That's what it is. Right?" (Sheff, 33, 117).

C H A P T E R   10

Paul Is Dead

And The Answer Is...

Obviously, many unanswered questions remain in the solution of the "Paul Is Dead" mystery. One of the first riddles involves the rumor's inception in Detroit, Michigan.

When the Beatles landed in America and attended their first press conference, the first question naturally was "When are you going to get a haircut?" The second question was, "What about the campaign in Detroit to stamp out the Beatles?" to which Paul responded, "We've got a campaign of our own to stamp out Detroit."

With this in mind, it seems both ironic and appropriate that the death rumors would leak from the city that sought the Beatles' end. The unknown mystery caller remains unidentified. Perhaps it was one of the Beatles themselves who broke the tragic news, or their press agent Derek Taylor who simply followed Paul's request to "Let it go." But, the rumor snowballed and gained momentum. *Sgt. Pepper's Lonely Heart's Club Band* was resurrected by the record-buying public as the search for the death clues intensified. *The White Album* and *Abbey Road* continued in album sales and brought in more revenue for the Apple coffers. Was it only a coincidence that Apple was in such dire financial trouble and the death clue hysteria helped generate the enormous amounts of income needed to meet the Beatles' everyday expenses and pay their debts?

If this were true, then the clever marketing of the death clues was extremely successful. Ironically, the trademark Apple itself referred back to the fall of man archetype since Adam had eaten from the forbidden tree of knowledge and cost man eternal paradise. The Beatles' self-chosen Apple resulted in the financial fall of the Beatles themselves.

If the Beatles had not considered the financial success of such a rumor, then perhaps they merely demonstrated their acceptance of Far

---

Eastern religious beliefs. In this case the Beatles could have provided clues to their being born-again into a new faith. This would explain the many references to the Eastern religious symbols and teachings.

Perhaps the whole controversy was only a coincidence. The readers only found clues that coincided with what they wanted to find. The seekers saw what they wanted to see and heard what they wanted to hear. However, there were far too many staged clues for an answer as simple as this.

Ideally, investigators should have stumbled onto the greatest hoax since the Halloween broadcast of Orson Welles' *The War Of The Worlds.* But, come to think of it, in which month were the clues first presented? The answer, of course, is October, the same month that Welles broadcast the supposed invasion of earth by Martians. The hysteria generated by both events are closely paralleled. The death clues are presented at the Halloween season -- a holiday that is not only famous for trick or treat but also associated with the death of the fertility god, the Fisher King.

Paul McCartney held his press conference in November to announce his well-being. Of course, November is the month of Thanksgiving, and a vast majority of the public gave thanks for McCartney's good health and decided that the "Paul Is Dead" rumor was merely a search by hysterical fans.

Since the month of December approached and visions of the Christmas season filled the public mind, it now appeared obvious that the symbolic cycle was now complete, since Christmas is associated with the birth of Christ. The choosing of the time frame could have been mere coincidence, but it fit with the concept of the Fisher King legend and helped fulfill the archetypal religious doctrine of birth, death, and rebirth, or in this case resurrection. In this way, Lennon could have easily demonstrated that at least, archetypally, the Beatles were every bit as popular as Jesus Christ to their worshipping audience.

If the Beatles did not stage a religious parody then perhaps the answer to the silence concerning the death clues lay in the investigation of the Charles Manson family. Today, there have been many attempts to hold rock groups accountable for their tremendous influence over adoring fans. Recently, civil lawsuits have been filed against Ozzy Osborne and Judas Priest concerning the effects of their songs upon impressionable, young fans. If rock lyrics and hidden messages result in a drastic change in human behavior, specifically attempted suicide, then the offending

---

musicians may very well be charged with numerous civil indictments. If found guilty of such a conspiracy, millions of dollars could be at stake.

Maybe it was just another coincidence that the "Paul Is Dead" rumors came to an abrupt halt during the highlights of the "Helter Skelter" murders. If the Beatles had admitted the presence of numerous hidden clues within their albums, perhaps they became concerned that they could very well be charged in some sort of conspiracy that would indirectly link them to the Manson murders. Had the group admitted that secret, sometimes subliminal, messages were planted to lead listeners on a Magical Mystery fantasy, then could Charles Manson's bizarre interpretations of Beatle lyrics lead to the group being involved in the California trial? Perhaps it would be much safer to give up the hoax and deny it ever happened. This way the Beatles would be safe from any lawsuit created to implicate the band members.

Maybe the joke was simply out of hand and it was better to cut their losses than risk any involvement by stating that cryptic clues and backward messages did exist on Beatle recordings.

One other puzzling thought lingered about the hoax concept. The Beatles, to this day, have stated that the whole search for the death clues was merely coincidence, and that the clues meant nothing. If a hoax was truly played upon the public, why haven't the surviving Beatles revealed the true details behind the hoax's conception? As the Christmas holiday season of 1969 passed quietly, and a new year presented itself filled with promise that the Vietnam War would soon end, and that the world would finally know world peace, American television sets glowed dimly on the cold Winter night of February 23, 1970, a little over six years since the Beatles had made their first appearance on *The Ed Sullivan Show.* The program, Rowan and Martin's *Laugh In,* presented the following skit in a scene involving two angels in Heaven:

Angel One: Is there any truth to the rumor that Paul McCartney is still alive?

Angel Two: I doubt it. Where do you think we get those groovy harp arrangements?

C H A P T E R 11

The Ultimate Beatle Death Clue Quiz

After reading the many clues in this book, it is time for you, dear reader, to try your hand at answering some trivia questions. See if you can earn your doctorate in Beatlemania by answering the following questions:

1. Where can the clue "Paul?" be found?
2. Give three interpretations for the fade out message at the conclusion of "Strawberry Fields Forever."
3. In which Beatles video does Ringo play a bass drum that reads "Love 3 Beatles"?
4. What did the term "walrus" supposedly represent to investigators?
5. What did the open hand over Paul's head on the cover of *Sgt. Pepper's Lonely Hearts Club Band* suggest?
6. Which famous attorney conducted a television hearing exploring the infamous death clues?
7. What was the day, month, and year of the tragic accident that claimed Paul McCartney?
8. Which DJ in Detroit, Michigan, broke the death clues to an unsuspecting world?
9. In which Beatle song can a listener hear Lennon state that "Paul Is Dead now, miss him, miss him, miss him!" (remember the track must be played backwards!)?
10. Who is Joe Ephgrave?
11. In which song does Ringo state, "You were in a car crash and you lost your hair"?
12. What is the importance of the message "BE AT LESO"?
13. Who was the mysterious girl Paul was with the night of the accident. Remember, he "took her home [and he] nearly made it"?

14. What is the symbolism behind the black walrus?

15. Give three reasons why John Lennon couldn't have been the walrus.

16. What automobile was McCartney driving the night of the accident? On which album jacket does this car appear?

17. What Shakespearean play is heard during the fade-out of "I am the Walrus"?

18. In which Beatle song does John Lennon sing of a mysterious victim who "blew his mind out in a car"?

19. George Harrison supposedly moans Paul's name over and over in the fade-out of which Beatle classic?

20. On "Revolution 9" the engineer's voice repeats "Number 9, Number 9" over and over. What does the voice say when the track is reversed?

21. Why is Paul's back turned to the camera on the backside of the *Sgt. Pepper's Lonely Hearts Club Band* album?

22. Give three clues that suggest that it is Paul in the black walrus suit on the cover of the *Magical Mystery Tour.*

23. What significance do the death clues borrow from Edgar Allen Poe, Lewis Carroll, William Shakespeare, Carl Jung, and James Joyce?

24. What is the symbolism behind the number nine? How does it relate to John Lennon?

25. What is the purpose of the line, "monsieur, monsieur, how about another one?"

26. Explain the importance of "LMW 28IF."

27. On which album cover do investigators claim a mysterious phone number is given to help explain the tragic fate of Paul McCartney?

28. Where is the hidden death's head on the back of the *Abbey Road* album?

29. Which death clue is associated with "connect the dots"?

30. What is the name of the mysterious double who took Paul McCartney's place?

31. Which investigator flew to England and claimed that the only way he would believe that Paul McCartney was still alive would be if Paul's fingerprints matched his 1965 passport?

32. Where do we find the death clue "I Was"?

33. Who knows "what it's like to be dead"?

34. What do the liner photos from *The White Album* seem to suggest?

35. How do the Beatle death clues relate to the Fisher King symbol?

36. In which Beatle song does John Lennon state that "one and one and one is three"?

37. Give the two death clues associated with *Life* magazine's cover photo and "The Magical McCartney Mystery" article.

38. Explain the hidden meaning behind the *Abbey Road* cover.

39. What interpretation is made of the *White Album*?

40. How many Beatle songs refer to mysterious car accidents?

41. Describe the hidden death clue behind the Beatles' *Yesterday and Today* album.

42. In which song does Lennon state that "the walrus was Paul"?

43. Which album cover contains a series of dots that when connected reveals the hidden message "3 Beatles"?

44. Compare the Beatle death clues to James Joyce's *Finnegan's Wake.*

45. What death clue is associated with *Rubber Soul?*

46. What death clue is associated with *Revolver?*

47. What role did Charles Manson play in hidden Beatle messages?

48. What message is spelled out in yellow hyacinth flowers on the *Sgt. Pepper's* cover?

49. Where is the line, "So alright Paul we had better go and see a surgeon" found?

50. Where can Paul be seen wearing a black carnation?

51. In this liner photo, Paul is seen lying back in a bathtub. This was supposed to represent McCartney as a headless corpse. Where is this photo found?

52. What is the significance of the OPD arm patch found on the inside of the *Sgt. Pepper's Lonely Hearts Club Band* album?

53. What color is the back of the *Sgt. Pepper's* album? What does this supposedly represent?

54. According to *Life* magazine, a sonogram was made comparing Paul's voice in separate vocal arrangements. What were the results of this study?

55. Where can a listener discern, "Get Me Out! Get Me Out!"?

56. What is the basic idea behind the conspiracy and cover-up involving the "Paul Is Dead" rumor?

57. Which song, played backward of course, seems to say "Turn Me On Dead Man?"

58. On which Beatle song fade-out can the following messages be heard: "Bury My Body," "Oh, Untimely Death," and "What? Is He Dead?"

59. In which Beatle song is Paul's double introduced for the first time?

----

60. What is the hidden meaning for the eggman's "goo goo goo joob"?
61. Where can one find Paul's bloody shoes?
62. Where can one find a blood-stained driving glove?
63. Where, on the *Sgt. Pepper's* cover, is the flaming car?
64. What is the meaning behind the *Let It Be* cover?
65. In which song does John ask us to "look through the bent back tulips"?
66. What is the purpose of John "fixing a hole in the ocean"?
67. What does the 1966 Beatles release *Oldies* suggest?
68. What clue suggests that the death hoax was intended for American audiences?
69. How do the songs "How Do You Sleep" and "Back Off Boogaloo" related to the "Paul Is Dead" conspiracy?
70. Give the coincidences behind Paul's *Red Rose Speedway, Flowers In the Dirt* and *Paul Is Live.*
71. What death clues are associated with the "Butcher Cover"?
72. What does the empty bowl of cherries from the *McCartney* solo album suggest?
73. Which Beatles song mentions a day when papers didn't come?
74. What similarities can be found connecting the "Paul Is Dead" rumor to the OJ Simpson case?
75. Where can a listener find the hidden message "Paul is bloody. . .Paul is very bloody"?
76. What is the irony behind Paul's barefoot walk across Abbey Road?
77. Name the city where the "Paul Is Dead" rumors began. Why is this significant?
78. What could Paul McCartney's solo album *Flowers In The Dirt* be a reference to?
79. What supposedly became of Jane Asher, Paul's one-time fiancée?
80. Cite one death clue on McCartney's *Off The Ground* album.
81. What is strange about the background of Paul's photograph on *Let It Be?*
82. What does each Beatle supposedly represent on *Abbey Road?*
83. What instrument does McCartney hold on the *Sgt. Pepper's* cover? Why is this unusual?
84. What did some sleuths make of Wings, the name of McCartney's band?
85. Give two explanations for Paul's position (facing the camera directly) on *Sgt. Pepper's.*

----

86. The end chord on *Sgt. Pepper's* is symbolic of what?
87. Where can McCartney be found in the fetal position?
88. What clues can be associated with "Apple"?
89. How are the drum from *Sgt. Pepper's* and the onion ("Glass Onion") similar? How does this relate to Lewis Carroll?
90. What is the imperfection in "BEATLES" on the back of *Abbey Road?*
91. Where does McCartney appear with scars above his upper lip?
92. Who was Billy Shears? What did many fans consider the mysterious name?
93. What is the M&D Company?
94. Where does Paul appear in a "coffin"?
95. Why did Paul grow a mustache for *Sgt. Pepper's?*
96. "Come Together" possibly refers to what scene?
97. What is significant about "Beatles" as opposed to "The Beatles"?
98. How do death clue researchers interpret the blurred image on the back of *Abbey Road?*
99. What is significant about the guitar strings on *Sgt. Pepper's?*
100. How did the epaulets the Beatles wear on *Sgt. Pepper's* contribute to the death clue hysteria?
101. Where does the image of the flaming car appear?

E P I L O G U E

It is difficult to imagine that it has now been over twenty-eight years ago today since "Sergeant Pepper taught the band to play." In 1992, Paul McCartney celebrated his fiftieth birthday. The colors silver and gold do well to describe the ageless melodic sounds of the still-Fab Four. Hopefully, my work will help encourage others to explore and enjoy the collected works of John Lennon, Paul McCartney, George Harrison, and Ringo Starr.

It is intriguing that the Beatles still refuse to comment upon their purpose in the formation of the death clues. Indisputably, McCartney continues to perpetuate the death clue rumors through his songs and album covers. (Some fans even suggested that the name of Paul McCartney's band, Wings, conjured up images of dying, angels, and heaven.) As proof of his willingness to incorporate hidden messages within his albums, McCartney included a message in Braille on his *Red Rose Speedway* album. The message, intended for Stevie Wonder, read, "We love you, Stevie, baby."

McCartney's album, *Flowers in the Dirt,* seemed to hint at a longing remembrance of a time of marching bands and girls with kaleidoscope eyes. Perhaps *Flowers In The Dirt* jokingly refers to the yellow hyacinth guitar placed upon a freshly-dug grave ("Paul?"). McCartney's album *Off The Ground* featured six pairs of bare feet, perhaps reminiscent of the famous walk across Abbey Road. In late 1993, McCartney released a new work entitled, appropriately enough, *Paul Is Live.* On the cover, Paul duplicates his infamous walk across Abbey Road. This time, instead of being part of a funeral procession, Paul is leading an English sheepdog across the notorious crosswalk. Perhaps there *is* a double in this picture. Not McCartney, however, but Martha, the sheepdog remembered fondly in "Martha My Dear." According to "Club Sandwich" this particular sheepdog's name is Arrow and belongs to Paul's son, James.

McCartney paid painstakingly close attention to every detail in creating this parody. The original *Abbey Road* photographer, Iain Macmillan, took the shot on July 22, 1993. Paul wore a suit made by Edward Sexton, the same tailor who made the suit he wore on the *Abbey Road* cover. The computer-generated scene (it was impossible to make the 'zebra' crossing stripes match the original photo) is complete with another Volkswagen Beetle parked alongside the curb with a license plate that reads "51 IS," which refers to the fact that Paul McCartney is still alive and rocking to this very day. But, in a world of computer generated graphics and high technology, anything is possible.

Almost twenty-six years to the day that the "Paul Is Dead" rumors appeared for the first time in the American media, Paul has chosen yet another format to display his humor concerning backward maskings and rumors of his tragic demise. Two episodes of *The Simpsons* hint at the rumor. (When Lisa Simpson first meets Paul McCartney, she tells him that she has heard about him in her history class.) The first episode, a Halloween special, features a tombstone etched with Paul McCartney's name. In the second episode, an animated Paul and Linda McCartney make a statement concerning their belief in vegetarianism. During the program, Paul states that playing "Maybe I'm Amazed" backwards will yield a "ripping recipe for lentil soup." Sure enough, at the song's conclusion, the fade-out features Paul singing "Maybe I'm Amazed" and, when reversed, the songs spells out the ingredients, cup by cup, with a dash of "Sgt. Pepper" to complete the popular vegetarian dish. And, during the backward mask, almost expectedly, he states, "Oh, by the way -- I'm alive."

A P P E N D I X

Rubber Soul: This album contained a sinister reference to "tires" (rubber) and "death" (soul); many fans felt that this reference suggested Paul's death in an automobile accident.

The Beatles Yesterday and Today: This American release hinted that a transition had taken place within the group and became the first of many strange coincidental album covers suggesting that Paul was dead. *The Beatles Yesterday and Today* contains the following clues:

1. Paul is sitting in an open trunk that resembles a coffin, especially when the cover is turned to the side.

2. Several of the song titles suggested that McCartney was tragically killed in a car accident, e.g. "Drive My Car," "Nowhere Man," "Dr. Robert," "Act Naturally," etc.

3. The album jacket may well hint at the first cover-up.

Revolver: The title suggested a change as in a revolving door: one person leaves as another enters. The album cover also suggested that Paul's photo was forced in with the others since his is in profile.

1. The lyrics to "She Said She Said" contains the mysterious line "I know what it's like to be dead."

2. In the song lyrics to "Got to Get You Into My Life" Paul sings, "I was alone, I took a ride, I didn't know what I would find there." There may well be a play on words when the singer suggests that he must get someone into his life. Could this mean that an impostor was brought in to take the place of the popular Beatle?

3. The song titles "I Wanna Tell You" and "Tomorrow Never Knows" hint at the supposed tragedy and an effort to reveal it to the public.

Sgt. Pepper's Lonely Hearts Club Band: This album was brimming with cryptic clues:

1. The Beatles stand above a grave on the cover.

2. The hyacinth flowers display a left-handed guitar [Paul's instrument]. The arrangement also spells out "Paul?"

3. The bass drum was designed by a Joe Ephgrave (an anagram for epitaph and grave.) When a mirror is placed in the center of "LONELY HEARTS" a hidden message is revealed: I ONE IX HE DIE. Interpreted, the message suggested that Eleven Nine [November the ninth] HE [McCartney since the points directly up at him] DIE. There is evidence that McCartney was actually involved in an automobile crash on this date.

4. On the album cover, there is an open hand above Paul's head. This was interpreted as a symbol of death.

5. The front cover displayed a doll wearing a "Welcome the Rolling Stones" sweatshirt. A model car, which resembled an Aston-Martin, the same type of car Paul was driving on the night of his tragic accident, rests on the doll's leg.

6. Paul is playing a black instrument, while the other members are playing golden ones.

7. When the album cover is opened, Paul's arm band displayed the letters OPD -- London police jargon for "Officially Pronounced Dead."

8. The back of the album cover is blood red, a color related to the tragic accident.

9. Paul's back is turned toward the camera striking a different pose (Many people believed that this was an impostor and according to some credible sources, they were right!)

10. The song title "Within You Without You" covers Paul's figure with the lyrics suggesting that "We never glimpse the truth until we pass away."

11. George is pointing at a line from the lyric "She's Leaving Home" which reads "Wednesday morning at five o'clock." This was taken to suggest the actual date and time of the accident. Strangely, November 9, 1966, was a Wednesday morning, and according to Beatle sources, Paul was involved in an accident on that day and at that precise time.

12. The title song introduced a mysterious Billy Shears who many fans thought was Paul's double. Some believed that he was a winner of a Paul McCartney look-alike contest while others thought "Billy Shears" was a pseudonym for William Campbell, an actor who, through plastic surgery, was able to take Paul's place in the group.

13. The composition "A Day In The Life" mentioned a person who "blew his mind out in a car. . .[who] hadn't noticed that the lights had changed. . .[while] a crowd of people stood and stared. They'd seen his face before." Was this a reference to Paul's accident? In this case, McCartney may have been decapitated and the viewing public failed to draw the connection to the famous group.

Magical Mystery Tour: What was the mystery that was "*dying* to take us away?"

1. The title of the LP, when held upside down and observed through a mirror, revealed a telephone number that supposedly enabled the viewer to find the truth about McCartney's death.

2. The Beatles are dressed in animal costumes, one of those being a black walrus which, in Scandinavian countries, is a symbol of death.

3. The rumor that the term "walrus" was from the Greek for "corpse" circulated wildly. Thus the song "I Am The Walrus" was translated as "I Am The Corpse."

4. In the lyrics to "I Am The Walrus":

a. Lennon sang "I am he as you are he as you are me and we are all together." Did this suggest that the Beatles conspired to hide McCartney's death and take his place in the recording studio?

b. Shakespearean actors recite lines from *King Lear* during the song's fade-out the lines include references to: "What. Is He Dead?" "Bury My Body!" "Oh! Untimely Death!"

5. During the fade-out and fade-in to "Strawberry Fields Forever" many fans heard an eerie voice exclaim "I Buried Paul!"

6. In the song booklet, there are scenes with Paul posed with hands over his head.

7. Paul sits behind a desk with a sign stating "I Was." He is in military dress and the British flags are crossed in the proper position for military funerals.

8. During the song "Your Mother Should Know," the Beatles descended a spiral staircase. John, George, and Ringo wore red carnations while Paul wore a black carnation, which many believed was another symbol of death.

----

9. The line "Goo goo goo joob" from "I Am the Walrus" is reportedly taken from James Joyce's *Finnegan's Wake* and was said to be the last words of the eggman [Humpty Dumpty] before his famous accident.

10. The lines from "I Am The Walrus": "Stupid bloody Tuesday" hinted at the night Paul angrily left Abbey Road studios right before the tragic accident early the next morning (Wednesday, November 9, 1966).

The White Album: This double LP contained the following clues:

1. The close-up photos of the Beatles differed again with Paul displaying mysterious scars around his upper lip that had not been noticed before. Were these the marks left behind by plastic surgery?

2. On the fold-out lyric sheet there is a picture of Paul lying back in a bath tub. Many felt that this suggested Paul's death, and that the waters that covered his neck again meant that he had been decapitated.

3. Again on the fold-out sheet, there is a photo of McCartney with eerie skeletal hands reaching out to ensnare him.

4. The soft muttering right before "Blackbird," when played backwards, seems to say "Paul is dead now, miss him, miss him, miss him!"

5. When "Revolution 9" is reversed, the listener hears the sounds of a flaming automobile crash with the victim screaming "Get Me Out!" The phrase "Number Nine" is reversed to reveal the passage "Turn Me On Deadman."

6. In the song "Glass Onion," John stated "Here's another clue for you all. . .the walrus was Paul!"

7. During "Don't Pass Me By," Ringo sang, "I'm sorry that I doubted you. I was so unfair. You were in a car crash and you lost your hair." This was taken as another reference to Paul's accidental death.

8. "Blackbirds" have always been symbolic of approaching death and disaster.

9. The color white represented the official color of mourning in many Far Eastern societies.

Abbey Road: The following clues are given:

1. The Beatles represented a funeral procession with Lennon being religion or God himself: Ringo, the church (minister) or perhaps the undertaker: Paul, the barefooted corpse, since many societies bury their dead without shoes, and George represented the gravedigger in his work clothes.

2. Paul is out of step with the others.

3. A Volkswagen Beetle's license plate read "28 IF," a reference to McCartney's age if he had lived.

4. The impostor Paul is holding a cigarette in his right hand, whereas the actual McCartney was left-handed.

5. The back of the album contained the term "Beatles" written on a wall. There is a small crack that ran through the "S" which suggested that there was a flaw within the band.

6. A series of dots before the Beatles sign, if connected, form the number three, which suggested that there were three Beatles (but there are four on the cover!)

7. There is a skull displayed in light and shadow and tilted at an angle following the Beatle sign.

8. The girl in the blue dress was said to be Jane Asher, Paul's long time fiancée, who was secretly paid not to reveal the terrible secret.

9. In the song "Come Together" Lennon sang, "One and one and one is three" which again referred to the Beatles as a three-man group.

10. The song "Come Together" may have referred to a wake held over a coffin when the mourners "come together over me!"

Let It Be: The last released Beatle album from 1970.

1. This album is designed in the appropriate color for a funeral -- black.

2. Notice that John, George, and Ringo are shown in profile, each looking to the left, whereas McCartney is photographed looking straight into the camera with a blood red background.

BIBLIOGRAPHY

Abrams, M.H. gen ed. *The Norton Anthology of English Literature.* W.W. Norton & Company, Inc. New York, 1968.

Brown, Peter and Stephen Gaines. *The Love You Make: An Insider's Story of the Beatles.* New American Library Penguin Books, New York, 1983.

Bugliosi, Vincent and Curt Gentry *Helter Skelter.* Bantam Books, New York, 1975.

Campbell, John and Henry Mordon Robinson. *A Skeleton Key to 'Finnegan's Wake'.* Harcourt Brace & Company, New York, 1944.

Carroll, Lewis. *The Complete Works of Lewis Carroll.* The Modern Library by Random House Inc., New York, 1916.

Cirlot, J.E. *Dictionary of Symbols.* -- trans. by Jack Sage. Philosophical Library, New York, 1971.

Coleman, Ray. *Lennon.* McGraw-Hill, New York, 1985.

Dowlding, William. *Beatle Songs.* Fireside by Simon & Schuster, New York, 1983.

Fawcett, Anthony. *John Lennon: One Day At A Time.* Grove Press, New York, 1976.

Fulpens, H.V. *The Beatles: An Illustrated Diary.* Perigree Books, New York, 1982.

Gaines, Steven. *Heroes and Villains: The True Story of the Beach Boys.* New American Library, 1986.

Gaskell, G.A. *Dictionary of all Scriptures and Myths.* Avenel Books, Julian Press, New York, 1981.

Goldman, Albert. The *Lives of John Lennon.* William Morrow & Company Inc., New York, 1988.

Harrison, George with Derek Taylor. *I Me Mine.* Simon and Schuster, New York, 1980.

Hockinson, Michael J. *The Ultimate Beatles Quiz Book.* St. Martin's Press, New York, 1992.

Jobes, Gertrude. *Dictionary of Mythology, Folklore, and Symbols. Part One.* The Scarecrow Press, Inc. New York, 1962.

Joyce, James. *Finnegan's Wake.* Viking Press, New York, 1939.

Lewisohn, Mark. *The Beatles: Recording Sessions.* Harmony Books, New York, 1988.

McCabe, Peter and Robert D. Schonfeld. *Apple to the Core.* Pocket Books, New York, 1972.

McCartney, Michael. *The Macs: Mike McCartney's Family Album.* Delilah Books, New York, 1972.

Marsh, David and Kevin Stein. *The Book Of Rock Lists.* Dell Rolling Stone Press, New York, 1981

Neary, John. 1969. The Magical McCartney Mystery. *Life,* 7 November, 103-5.

Norman, Philip. *Shout! The Beatles in Their Generation.* Warner Books, New York, 1982.

Poundstone, William. *Big Secrets.* Quill, New York, 1983.

Riley, Tim. *Tell Me Why: A Beatles Commentary.* Alfred A. Knopt, New York, 1988.

Salewicz, Tim. *McCartney.* St. Martin's Press, New York, 1986.

Schaffner, Nicholas. *The Beatles Forever.* McGraw-Hill, New York, 1978.

Schultheiss, Tom. *A Day In The Life: The Beatles Day By Day.* Pierian Press, Michigan, 1980.

Sheff, David. *The Playboy Interviews With John Lennon & Yoko Ono.* Berkley Books, New York, 1981.

Shotton, Pete with Nicholas Shaffner. *The Beatles, Lennon, And Me.* Stein And Day, New York, 1984.

Stannard, Neville. *The Long and Winding Road: A History of the Beatles on Record.* Avon Books, New York, 1984.

Suczek, Barbara. 1972. The Curious Case of the Death of Paul McCartney. *Urban Life and Culture.* Vol. 1. Sage Publications.

Taylor, Derek. *It Was Twenty Years Ago Today.* Fireside, New York, 1987.

All lyrics written by the Beatles and credited where used: Lennon and McCartney; Harrison; Starr.

"A Day In The Life" words and music by John Lennon and Paul McCartney. Album: *Sgt. Pepper's Lonely Hearts Club Band* © Northern Songs, 1967.
"Baby You're a Rich Man" words and music by John Lennon and Paul McCartney. Album: *The Magical Mystery Tour* © Northern Songs, 1967.
"Back Off Boogaloo" words and music by Richard Starkey. Album: *Blast From Your Past* © Startling Music, Ltd., 1972.
"Blackbird" words and music by John Lennon and Paul McCartney. Album: *The Beatles (The White Album)* © Northern Songs, 1968.
"Blue Jay Way" words and music by George Harrison. Album: The *Magical Mystery Tour* © Northern Songs, 1967.
"Come Together" words and music by John Lennon and Paul McCartney. Album: *Abbey Road* © Northern Songs, 1969.

"Don't Pass Me By" words and music by Ringo Starr. Album: *The Beatles* (*The White Album*) © Sterling Music Limited, 1968.

"Drive My Car" words and music by John Lennon and Paul McCartney. Album: *Yesterday and Today* © Northern Songs, 1965.

"Glass Onion" words and music by John Lennon and Paul McCartney. Album: *The Beatles* (*The White Album*) © Northern Songs, 1968.

"Good Morning Good Morning" words and music by John Lennon and Paul McCartney. Album: *Sgt. Pepper's Lonely Hearts Club Band* © Northern Songs, 1967.

"Got To Get You Into My Life" words and music by John Lennon and Paul McCartney. Album: *Revolver* © Northern Songs, 1966.

"Happiness Is A Warm Gun" words and music by John Lennon and Paul McCartney. Album: *The Beatles* (*The White Album*) © Northern Songs, 1968.

"Hello Goodbye" words and music John Lennon and Paul McCartney. Album: *The Magical Mystery Tour* © Northern Songs, 1967.

"Helter Skelter" words and music by John Lennon and Paul McCartney. Album: *The Beatles* (*The White Album*) © Northern Songs, 1968.

"Honey Pie" words and music by John Lennon and Paul McCartney. Album: *The Beatles* (*The White Album*) © Northern Songs, 1968.

"How Do You Sleep" words and music by John Lennon & Yoko Ono. Album: *Imagine* © Maclen Ono Music, 1971.

"I Am The Walrus" words and music by John Lennon and Paul McCartney. Album: *The Magical Mystery Tour* © Northern Songs, 1967.

"I'm So Tired" words and music by John Lennon and Paul McCartney. Album: *The Beatles* (*The White Album*) © Northern Songs, 1968.

"Lovely Rita" words and music by John Lennon and Paul McCartney. Album: *Sgt. Pepper's Lonely Hearts Club Band* © Northern Songs, 1967.

"Magical Mystery Tour" words and music by John Lennon and Paul McCartney. Album: *The Magical Mystery Tour* © Northern Songs, 1967.

"Piggies" words and music by George Harrison. Album: *The Beatles* (*The White Album*) © Harrisongs Limited, 1968.

"Revolution" words and music by John Lennon and Paul McCartney. Album: *The Beatles* (*The White Album*) © Northern Songs, 1968.

"Revolution 9" words and music by John Lennon and Paul McCartney. Album: *The Beatles* (*The White Album*) © Northern Songs, 1968.

"Sexy Sadie" words and music by John Lennon and Paul McCartney. Album: *The Beatles* (*The White Album*) © Northern Songs, 1968.

"Sgt. Pepper's Lonely Hearts Club Band" words and music by John Lennon and Paul McCartney. Album: *Sgt. Pepper's Lonely Hearts Club Band* © Northern Songs, 1967.

"She Said She Said" words and music by John Lennon and Paul McCartney. Album: *Revolver* © Northern Songs, 1966.

"She's Leaving Home" words and music by John Lennon and Paul McCartney. Album: *Sgt. Pepper's Lonely Hearts Club Band* © Northern Songs, 1967.

"Strawberry Fields Forever" words and music by John Lennon and Paul McCartney. Album: *Magical Mystery Tour* © Northern Songs, 1967.

"While My Guitar Gently Weeps" words and music by George Harrison. Album: *The Beatles* (*The White Album*) © Harrisongs Limited, 1968.

"With A Little Help From My Friends" words and music by John Lennon and Paul McCartney. Album: *Sgt. Pepper's Lonely Hearts Club Band* © Northern Songs, 1967.

"Within You Without You" words and music by George Harrison. Album: *Sgt. Pepper's Lonely Hearts Club Band* © Northern Songs, 1967.

To order additional
copies of
The Walrus Was Paul,
call
1-800-409-7277
or write:

Dowling Press
3200 West End Avenue
Suite 500
Nashville, TN 37203

About the author

R. Gary Patterson teaches high school literature and lives with his wife Delores in Oliver Springs, Tennessee.